GCSE ENGLISH
FOR EDEXCEL
TEACHER'S RESOURCE

SERIES EDITOR: **Peter Ellison**

ANDREW LIDDLE

RICHARD ORMROD

SHIRLEY ORMROD

Hodder & Stoughton
A MEMBER OF THE HODDER HEADLINE GROUP

Acknowledgements:

The authors and publishers would like to thank the following for their kind permission to reproduce copyright material:

Copyright Text: p. 80 extract from *The Lady in the Van* by Alan Bennett © Faber and Faber; p. 134 article from the *Daily Express*; p. 135 two articles from the *Daily Telegraph*; p. 139 article from The *Daily Telegraph*; p. 146 article from *The Times*; p. 147 article from the *Daily Mirror*; p. 160 article from the *Daily Telegraph*; p. 161 extract from British Rail leaflet; p. 164 and 165 extracts from *A Gun for Sale* by Graham Greene, published by Victor Gollancz, an imprint of Orion; p. 167 article from The *Daily Telegraph* p. 171 article from *The Times*; p. 172 article from *The Times*.

Copyright photographs: p. 139 © PA Photos; p. 147 two photos © Solent News and Photo Agency; p. 156 © Andrew Ward/Life File; p. 167 © R D Battersby/Tografox.

Copyright artworks: pp. 113, 114, 117 Philip Page; p. 184 The British Railway board (artist's name unknown); pp. 5, 24, 37, 44, 56, 108 Ruth Thomlevold; pp. 3 and 136 Adrian Barclay.

Orders: please contact Bookpoint Ltd, 130 Milton Park, Abingdon, Oxon OX14 4SB. Telephone (44) 01235 827720. Fax: (44) 01235 400454. Lines are open from 9.00–6.00, Monday to Saturday, with a 24 hour message answering service. You can also order through our website www.hodderheadline.co.uk.

British Library Cataloguing in Publication Data
A catalogue record for this title is available from the British Library

ISBN 0 340 85746 3

First Published 2003
Impression number   10 9 8 7 6 5 4 3 2 1
Year   2007 2006 2005 2004 2003

Typeset by Fakenham Photosetting Limited, Fakenham, Norfolk.
Printed in Great Britain for Hodder & Stoughton Educational, a division of Hodder Headline, 338 Euston Road, London NW1 3BH by Hobbs the Printers, Totton, Hampshire.

CONTENTS

INTRODUCTION iv

SECTION A: READING

UNIT 1: Modern Poetry 1
    Collection A: In Such a Time As This 11
    Collection B: Identity 28
    Collection C: Nature 45

UNIT 2: Non-fiction Prose 62

UNIT 3: Different Cultures and Traditions 89

UNIT 4: Shakespeare – Macbeth 111

UNIT 5: Media 127

SECTION B: WRITING

UNIT 6: Writing to Argue, Persuade, Advise 149

UNIT 7: Writing to Inform, Explain, Describe 159

UNIT 8: Writing to Analyse, Review, Comment . . 166

UNIT 9: Pre-1914 text 174
    Poetry 174
    Prose 198

INTRODUCTION

The *GCSE English for Edexcel: Teacher's Resource* is designed to be used in conjunction with the Student's Book and provides teachers with photocopiable resources to support every aspect of the GCSE English course and all aspects of the English Literature course, except Modern Prose and Drama.

Each unit begins with a 'Using this Unit' page which explains how the subsequent material can best be used. The poetry section, for instance, contains general advice about tackling poetry in the exam as well as individual revision sheets on each of the poems. These raise questions designed to enable students to respond to the poem, followed by Foundation and Higher Tier exam questions.

As well as supporting each unit of the Student's Book, this resource includes selections of suitable pre-1914 poetry and prose suitable for foundation and higher candidates. It also includes an alternative Shakespeare unit, which focuses on *Macbeth*.

The *GCSE English for Edexcel: Teacher's Resource* contains extension tasks designed for more able students and further assignments for students to work on in their own time as part of their revision. This ensures that there is continuity between the work students do in class and their revision as they approach the exams.

Although this resource does not cover the speaking and listening requirements explicitly, every unit contains suitable EN1 assignments, which teachers can use as the basis for assessment.

All opportunities for 'Speaking and Listening' Practice and Assessment are indicated by:

All examples of 'Exam Practice' questions and essays at both Foundation and Higher Tier are indicated by:

Activities and assignments requiring Writing are marked by the following icon:

Activities and assignments marked by the following icon require Thinking only:

1 Modern Poetry

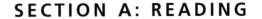

The Specifications

For both English A (1203) and B (1204) Paper 2F/AH (The Craft of the Writer, Part A) and for English Literature (1213) Paper 2F/3H, Part A, students will be examined on their knowledge and understanding of one of the three Modern Poetry collections in *The Edexcel Anthology for GCSE English*:

> Collection A: In Such a Time as This
> Collection B: Identity
> Collection C: Nature.

✱ They may use the same collection of poems for both English and English Literature.

However, there are some important differences to remember, especially that:

✱ Questions will address different named poems in the two exams.

✱ The Assessment Objectives are different (see below):

English A (1203); B (1204)
Question Styles

1 Choice of *two* questions.

2 One will name *two* or more poems; the other will name *one* and ask you to choose one or two more.

Assessment Objectives

✱ Students are required to read with insight and engagement, making appropriate references to texts and developing and sustaining their interpretations.

✱ They are further required to understand and evaluate how writers use linguistic, structural and presentational devices to achieve their effects; and to comment on the ways language varies and changes.

English Literature (1213)
Question Styles

1 Choice of two questions.

2 One will name *two* or more poems and ask you to choose one or two more.

3 English Literature questions on the poems, unlike the English questions, will always ask for comparison.

> ### *Assessment Objectives*
>
> * Students are expected to respond to texts critically, sensitively and in detail; select appropriate ways to convey response and to use textual evidence.
>
> * They are also expected to explore relationships and comparisons between texts; select and evaluate relevant material.

It is necessary to teach all the poems in the collection – although for questions in both the English and English Literature examinations students will be focusing on just two (or three) poems from one of the collections. The questions will obviously be concerned with the named theme and will require them to write lengthily and exploratively about:

* The content of the poems: their meanings, themes, the message each poet is trying to put over to the reader.

* The language of the poems: the words, phrases, sentences and images the poets use.

* The presentation of the poems: how they are set out, what kind of verse patterns they have, their rhyme and rhythm, and so on.

For the English Literature examination they will have to make comparisons between the poems. In order to do this they will need to see clearly the features the poems have in common and be able to make cross-references.

All of these considerations have been dealt with in the Student's Book – and the work in the Teacher's Resource has been designed to complement it.

The specifications of both subjects, English and English Literature, are crying out for the students to read the texts closely and engage with them. They need to be encouraged to treat the poems in a hands-on way, playing around with them, picking up a line or two here, an image there, 'squeezing' the meaning out.

The poems in the three collections have been grouped into themes, which means the student will be looking at poems that can be fairly easily compared with those around them. When working through the Student's Book they will be focusing on what makes a particular poem interesting and appealing. Although to a large extent these are matters for the student to decide, it is useful for them to think of there being five basic areas of involvement with a poem:

* Its content – what it means.

* Its language – the words used and the imagery created.

* Its form – the rhyme and the rhythm.

* Its mood – the feelings created.

* Its theme – the central ideas.

There are also opportunities for 'Writing based on the Poem' which represent 'Personal and Imaginative Writing' coursework. Here, in the Teacher's Resource, there are also Worksheets that lead up to practice essays very similar to the actual exams, which will help the student to gain valuable experience.

Students must be encouraged not to agonise over a poem, thinking it must be difficult or have a very deep meaning. They should understand that there is no law that says a particular poem has only one particular meaning. In fact, different people will 'read' it in different ways. The main thing is for the student to be able to support whatever view they happen to have, and the best way of doing this is by quotation.

They do need to be actively encouraged to think of quotation as the best way to 'engage' with the poem – to get involved with it. Give them this state-of-the-art method to help them with the art of stating and, more importantly, SHOWING what they mean:

a) Introduce a point, for example that the poet has used a particular simile to put a striking image in your mind. Briefly put this simile in its context, i.e. where it stands in relation to the overall meaning and flow of thought.

b) Quote the simile, using quotation marks. If it's more than a line in length, put it on a new line in a central position.

c) And now, very importantly, reinforce the point being proved, by adding to the quote, explaining how it works, what it means, how it contributes to the overall effect.

Tell them that they won't half impress the examiner if they use this method. Tell them to grapple or wrestle with the language the poet has actually used – and to remember, conversely, that they will not impress anybody if they simply feature-spot, for example, 'There is some alliteration in line 2'.

They should never be afraid to develop their own ideas, however. Encourage them to think about the 'sound' the poem makes when read aloud. What ideas does the poem give them? What attitude does the poet appear to have towards the subject matter? What, then, overall, is the student's attitude towards the poem? All of these issues should quite properly come out as they answer the exam questions.

FURTHER USEFUL TIPS TO PASS ON:

1 Try to gain a good working knowledge of all sixteen poems in the collection studied as different ones will be named in each exam.

2 Practise the specimen essays across a range of the poems.

3 Make comparisons between different poems, not just the same ones.

4 Make sure that you understand basic literary terms (for example, metaphor, simile, alliteration, onomatopoeia, enjambment), and why and how poets use them.

5 Let yourself enjoy the poems as well as studying them for exams!

Modern Poetry: Teacher's Notes

Using this Unit: this page of teacher's notes sets out how to make optimum use of this set of resources. *See page 7*

Oral Coursework Interviews: this represents extension work to the poem 'You Will Be Hearing From Us Shortly' by U.A. Fanthorpe. It is a useful and effective piece of Oral Coursework. It is popular with the class and is a good piece of pairs coursework.

Modern Poetry: Resource Worksheets, Handouts and OHTs

Tackling a Poem

These photocopiable sheets take the students through three stages, leading to in-depth knowledge and understanding. They provide an introduction by using examples from **all three collections of poetry** in *The Edexcel Anthology for GCSE English*; and an indication of some of the technical terms needed.

1a. **'How to Tackle a Poem' OHT:** this OHT provides the basis for a series of lessons, taking the students through a range of skills and technical terms required in poetic analysis. *See page 8*

1b. **'Language Chart' Worksheet:** this photocopiable worksheet provides a framework for students to keep a record of the skills learned and applied to specific poems. This will, later, be invaluable for revision. *See page 9*

1c. **'Understanding the Poems' Worksheet:** students need to complete one of these for each of the sixteen poems in either Collection A, B or C of Unit 1 Modern Poetry. *See page 10*

These worksheets and OHTs are intended to supplement the information given in the Student's Book, to be a handy source of information and to provide the opportunity for students to gather, organise and record information. 1a. 'How to Tackle a Poem' OHT, in particular, provides invaluable visual illustration of key points.

Here are 48 photocopiable handouts containing a set of preparation questions and an essay question (and an alternative essay for the foundation tier) on each of the sixteen poems from each collection.

Collection A

Childhood Memories

1Aa. '"Half-past Two" by U.A. Fanthorpe' Handout *See page 12*

1Ab. '"Hide and Seek" by Vernon Scannell' Handout *See page 13*

1Ac. '"Brendon Gallacher" by Jackie Kay' Handout *See page 14*

1Ad. '"Lucozade" by Jackie Kay' Handout *See page 15*

1Ae. '"Yellow" by Jackie Kay' Handout *See page 16*

1Af. '"The House" by Matthew Sweeney' Handout *See page 17*

New Beginnings

1Ag. '"Wherever I Hang" by Grace Nichols' Handout *See page 18*

1Ah. '"Where the Scattering Began" by Merle Collins' Handout *See page 19*

1Ai. '"The Darkling Thrush" by Thomas Hardy' Handout *See page 20*

1Aj. '"Electricity Comes to Cocoa Bottom" by Mercia Douglas' Handout *See page 21*

1Ak. '"You Will Be Hearing From Us Shortly" by U.A. Fanthorpe' Handout *See page 22*

War and Death

1Al. '"Refugee Blues" by W.H. Auden' Handout *See page 23*

1Am. '"War Music" by Christopher Logue' Handout *See page 24*

1An. '"The Send-off" by Wilfred Owen' Handout *See page 25*

1Ao. '"Dulce et Decorum Est" by Wilfred Owen' Handout *See page 26*

1Ap. '"Death in Leamington" by John Betjeman' Handout *See page 27*

Collection B

Old Age

1Ba. '"Warning" by Jenny Joseph' Handout *See page 29*

1Bb. '"Mirror" by Sylvia Plath' Handout *See page 30*

1Bc. '"Old Man, Old Man" by U.A. Fanthorpe Handout *See page 31*

1Bd. '"Follower" by Seamus Heaney' Handout *See page 32*

1Be. '"At Grass" by Philip Larkin' Handout *See page 33*

Moments of Decision or Realisation

1Bf. '"I Shall Paint my Nails Red" by Carole Satyamurti' Handout *See page 34*

1Bg. '"Once Upon a Time" by Gabriel Okara' Handout *See page 35*

1Bh. '"Death of a Naturalist" by Seamus Heaney' Handout *See page 36*

1Bi. '"The Road Not Taken" by Robert Frost' Handout *See page 37*

1Bj. '"Mid-Term Break' by Seamus Heaney' Handout *See page 38*

Individual Experience

1Bk. ' "Miracle on St David's Day' by Gillian Clarke' Handout *See page 39*

1Bl. '"The Barn' by Seamus Heaney' Handout *See page 40*

1Bm. '"An Unknown Girl" by Moniza Alvi' Handout *See page 41*

1Bn. '"Not My Best Side" by U.A. Fanthorpe' Handout *See page 42*

1Bo. '"Still I Rise" by Maya Angelou' Handout *See page 43*

1Bp. '"Digging" by Seamus Heaney' Handout *See page 44*

Collection C

Encounters with the Natural World

1Ca. '"The Horses" by Edwin Muir' Handout *See page 46*

1Cb. '"The Thought-Fox" by Ted Hughes' Handout *See page 47*

1Cc. '"The Stag" by Ted Hughes' Handout *See page 48*

1Cd. '"Roe-Deer" by Ted Hughes' Handout *See page 49*

1Ce. '"Break of Day in the Trenches" by Isaac Rosenberg' Handout *See page 50*

The Power of Nature

1Cf. '"Wind" by Ted Hughes' Handout *See page 51*

1Cg. '"Mushrooms" by Sylvia Plath' Handout *See page 52*

1Ch. '"The Storm" by Theodore Roethke' Handout *See page 53*

1Ci. '"Thistles" by Ted Hughes' Handout *See page 54*

1Cj. '"Trout" by Seamus Heaney' Handout *See page 55*

Nature and Change

1Ck. '"Iguana Memory" by Grace Nichols' Handout *See page 56*

1Cl. '"Keeping Orchids" by Jackie Kay' Handout *See page 57*

1Cm. '"Nettles" by Vernon Scannell' Handout *See page 58*

1Cn. '"The Flowers" by Selima Hill' Handout *See page 59*

1Co. '"The Five Students" by Thomas Hardy' Handout *See page 60*

1Cp. '"A Blade of Grass" by Brian Patten' Handout *See page 61*

Using this Unit

Before reading the poems show students 'How to tackle a poem' OHT on page 8. Also read through with them pages 2–5 in the Student's Book (beginning with the header: 'Tackling a Poem'), so that they are aware of what to look out for when they begin studying the individual poems. Explain thoroughly the technical terms encountered.

See pages 8–10

The two worksheets will be useful for establishing the students' understanding of the poems. These should be photocopied and distributed as the poems are studied. 'Understanding the Poems' Worksheet requires them to answer the important questions brought to their attention in the Student's Book, 'Tackling a Poem' (pages 2–5). 'Language Chart' Worksheet is designed to make students more aware of the conscious decisions about language made by the writers.

Collection A: See pages 11–27

Collection B: See pages 28–44

Collection C: See pages 45–61

Here you will find 48 photocopiable handouts that contain a set of questions and an exam practice essay (and alternative essay for the foundation tier) on each of the sixteen poems from Collections A, B and C.

These are revision exercises to be completed at the end of the course, although, alternatively, they can be used whilst studying the poems to further aid the students as they work through the poems.

1a HOW TO TACKLE A POEM

* Read the poem aloud, to experience its **rhyme**, **rhythm** and **alliteration**.

* Read it two or three times to understand its **content** because it is much more intense and condensed than prose.

* Read it once more aloud to capture its **tone**.

* Understand its **content** – where it's set.

* Understand its **theme** – the ideas or issues being expressed.

* Be aware of its **mood** – the emotions and atmosphere.

* Understand its **structure** – is it in verses or is some other way used to separate ideas?

* Understand the **language** and **imagery** – why the poet has chosen particular words and phrases. (Never let a good **metaphor** or **simile** pass you by!)

* Be aware there is no one single 'reading' of a poem – your response is as valid as anyone else's, as long as you can support it with **evidence**.

* The evidence lies in your **quotations** and how you comment on them.

* Never just describe and narrate – always say **why** and **how** a poet uses language.

1b

LANGUAGE CHART

Make a note of examples of poetic language you find particularly interesting, explaining the type of poetic device (for example, metaphor or alliteration) used and how it works.

Title of poem . . . .

QUOTATION	POETIC DEVICE	HOW IT WORKS

1c UNDERSTANDING THE POEMS

Having read the poem, begin to fill in this chart which will help you recognise and understand the key components of the poem. You can return to this chart and add more as your knowledge of the poem grows.

Title of poem . . . .

QUESTIONS	RESPONSES
What do you think is the significance of the title?	
What is the tone of the poem? Is it serious or humorous?	
What type of poem is it? Does it tell a story, express ideas, or both?	
What is the central theme of the poem? Is there more than one theme?	
What is the mood of the poem? How does it make you feel? Do you think the author intended you to feel like this?	
What would you say is the poet's viewpoint (the way he or she sees the issue or idea expressed in the poem)?	
Does the poem have a particular form? Is the poem in verses? Why has the poet chosen to arrange the material as it is? Does it suit the subject matter?	
Is there a rhyme scheme or rhythm? If so how does it work?	
What type of language does the author use? Give examples. Do you find it effective?	
Do you like the poem? Why (or why not)?	

(Collection A:) In Such a Time as This

You will need to teach all the poems in *Collection A: In Such a Time as This*, although for the questions in both the English and English Literature examinations students will be focusing on just two (or three) poems. The questions will obviously be concerned with the theme of *In Such a Time as This* and will require them to write lengthily and exploratively about:

* ✱ The content of the poems: their meanings, themes, the message each poet is trying to put over to the reader.
* ✱ The language of the poems: the words, phrases, sentences and images each poet uses.
* ✱ The presentation of the poems: how they are set out, what kind of verse patterns they have, their rhyme and rhythm, and so on.

For the English Literature examination they will have to make comparisons between the poems. In order to do this they will need to see clearly the features the poems have in common and be able to make cross-references.

All of these considerations have been dealt with in the Student's Book – and the work in this Teacher's Resource has been designed to complement it.

1Aa. 'HALF-PAST TWO' BY U.A. FANTHORPE

Essay Preparation

In pairs, discuss and make brief notes in response to the following questions.

1 List all the times that are important to the child.

2 What does the child mean by 'the little eyes' and 'two long legs for walking' when he describes the clock face? Why do you think he uses this type of description?

3 'Click' is an unusual word for the sound of a clock. What word do we usually use? What do they both have in common?

4 What other connotation does 'click' have in this poem?

5 What had the child 'escaped' from?

6 In the eighth verse he lists what he had escaped 'into'. What are these three things?

7 Why does the poet use italics in the ninth verse?

8 What 'times' was he 'slotted back into'?

9 Do you think he was disappointed to have to come back into the 'real' world?

10 Put the following in your own words:
'. . . once by not knowing time,
He escaped into the clockless land of ever,
Where time hides tick-less waiting to be born.'

EXAM PRACTICE ESSAYS

Essay

'Half-Past Two' is a poem about a child's feelings when left alone. Look at 'Hide and Seek' by Vernon Scannell in which a child has a similar, but different, experience. By comparing the two poems, show which of the two writers seems to you to convey ideas more successfully.

 Remember to support your answer with examples from the texts.

Foundation Tier Essay

Look again at 'Half-Past Two' and *one* other poem from **Collection A: In Such a Time as This**. How do the writers of the two poems help you to understand the events or incidents they describe? For each poem you should write about:

* the details of the scene
* the feelings of the people
* the poet's use of language.

 Remember to support your answer with examples from each text.

1Ab.   HIDE AND SEEK BY VERNON SCANNELL

Essay Preparation

In pairs, discuss and make brief notes in response to the following questions.

1   What is the child's first action in the poem?

2   What do the sacks smell of?

3   Why is it wiser not to 'risk' another shout?

4   In lines 6–7, what does he think the other children are doing?

5   When the seekers do come what does the child think is odd about their actions?

6   Why do you think 'their words and laughter scuffle'? What are they laughing about? What does 'scuffle' normally describe?

7   In line 16, what does the boy believe the seekers are thinking about him?

8   What four things worry him in lines 18–20?

9   Why does the boy think he is the 'winner'? What does he want 'them' to do?

10   What, in fact, has happened? What do you think about their 'trick'?

EXAM PRACTICE ESSAYS

Essay

In 'Hide and Seek' and 'Brendon Gallacher' by Jackie Kay, both boys experience a painful moment of growing up. Compare the way in which the poets have described this experience. Which do you find the most effective?

 Remember to support your answer with examples from the texts.

Foundation Tier Essay

Look again at 'Hide and Seek' and *one* other poem in **Collection A: In Such a Time as This**.

How have the poets made the incidents or events they describe come alive for you? For each poem you should write about:

✱   the description of events
✱   the characters' feelings and attitudes
✱   the poet's use of language.

 Remember to support your answer with examples from each text.

13

1Ac. 'BRENDON GALLACHER' BY JACKIE KAY

Essay Preparation

In pairs, discuss and make brief notes in response to the following questions.

1 Which countries did the young girl and Brendon come from?

2 Where was Brendon's father and why do you think he was there?

3 What was the child's father's job?

4 How many brothers did they each have?

5 Copy out the phrases that tell us that Brendon was both kind and protective towards the child.

6 What did Brendon plan for his mother 'when he got older'?

7 What excuse does the girl give when her mother tells her to ask Brendon 'round to dinner'?

8 How long had they been 'friends' for?

9 How does the poet make Brendon's appearance so vivid, when she mourns his 'death'?

10 Find two examples of colloquial language in the poem. What do they add to it?

EXAM PRACTICE ESSAYS

Essay

The girl has a close relationship with her imaginary friend, Brendon. Compare this relationship with that of the girl and her mother in 'Lucozade', a poem also by Jackie Kay.

 Remember to support your answer with examples from the texts.

Foundation Tier Essay

Look again at 'Brendon Gallacher' and *one* other poem in **Collection A: In Such a Time as This**.

How do the writers of the two poems help you to understand the events or incidents they describe?

For each poem you should write about:

✳ the events that took place
✳ the feelings of the people
✳ the poet's use of language.

 Remember to support your answer with examples from each text.

14

1Ad. 'LUCOZADE' BY JACKIE KAY

Essay Preparation

In pairs, discuss and make brief notes in response to the following questions.

1 What four things does the mother say she does not want?

2 What does she want? Would they be good for her?

3 In the second verse, 'She nods off and her eyes go back in her head', who is making this comment and what does it mean?

4 In the third verse she tells her daughter about her day. Notice that the first two lines tell us how she is. Which two words in these two lines are most effective?

5 What does the mother mean when she says 'Grapes have no imagination, they're just green'?

6 In the sixth verse the girl takes everything home from 'her cupboard in ward 10B, Stobhill Hospital.' What effect does giving all the details about the hospital have?

7 The seventh verse is less straightforward. What words in it have ideas or connotations of heaven?

8 We know that the mother is happy now: she seems released, her sheets 'billow and whirl'. Why do you think this happens?

9 What do you think 'dandelion hours' means?

10 Why do you think the girl is 'singing an old song'?

 EXAM PRACTICE ESSAYS

Essay

Compare 'Lucozade' with 'Yellow' in which Jackie Kay also discusses family relationships. Which poem do you prefer and why?

 Remember to support your answer with examples from the texts.

Foundation Tier Essay

Look again at 'Lucozade' and *one* other poem from **Collection A: In Such a Time as This**.

How have the poets described the scenes, places and characters they are writing about? For each poem you should write about:

✱ the description of events
✱ the characters' feelings and attitudes
✱ the poet's use of language.

Remember to support your answer with examples from each text.

15

1Ae. **'YELLOW' BY JACKIE KAY**

Essay Preparation

In pairs, discuss and make brief notes in response to the following questions.

1 Why do you think this poem is called 'Yellow' instead of 'My Family'?

2 What season does it appear to be in the first verse?

3 List all the references to things 'yellow' in the poem and say what they add to it.

4 Piece together what we learn about the poet's mother from the poem.

5 What is the significance of the parts in the poem that are in italics?

6 What impressions do you get of the poet's father and brother?

7 Which of the visitors in the second verse sounds the most unpleasant? Explain why.

8 Comment as fully as possible on the last line of the poem.

9 Why might a 'yellow pineapple ring' be described as 'happy'?

10 Imagine that the poem is to be the basis for a new soap opera on TV. Write notes on each character mentioned, adding ideas of your own which you think would fit.

 EXAM PRACTICE ESSAYS

Essay

Look again at 'Yellow' and *one* other poem from the **Childhood Memories** section of *Collection A: In Such a Time as This*. How do the poets bring these experiences in these poems to life?

Remember to support your answer with examples from the texts.

Foundation Tier Essay

Look again at 'Yellow' and 'Lucozade'. How does Jackie Kay show relationships between adults and children?

For each poem you should write about:

✱ the behaviour of the adults
✱ how the adults affect the children
✱ the poet's use of language.

Remember to support your answer with examples from each text.

1Af. **'THE HOUSE' BY MATTHEW SWEENEY**

Essay Preparation

In pairs, discuss and make brief notes in response to the following questions.

1 How many bedrooms did the house have? What did the poet dislike about the bedrooms?

2 What does he mean by using the word 'scouts' to describes the rats' actions? What makes 'scouts' an ironic word to use?

3 What had 'never' happened at the house? Look at the repetition of the word 'never' in lines 16, 19 and 27. What effect does this have?

4 What happened to the cockroaches when they came out after dark? What does this tell us about the dog?

5 What were the crows said to be 'planning'?

6 What sometimes happened to the crows?

7 Why do you think 'neighbours never entered/as often'?

8 What word tells us that he thought of the 'piano' and the fact that he grew up in the house in a different way from the other things he described?

9 Do you think the poet had a happy or unhappy childhood?

10 Would you like to have grown up in that house? Give your reasons.

EXAM PRACTICE ESSAYS

Essay

Compare Matthew Sweeney's depiction of childhood in 'The House' with that described in 'Yellow' by Jackie Kay.

How does the poets' choice of words in these two poems convey the strength of his or her feelings about the atmosphere and the events portrayed? Which choice of words do you think is the most effective?

 Remember to support your answer with examples from the texts.

Foundation Tier Essay

Look again at 'The House' and compare it with *one* other poem in **Collection A: In Such a Time as This**. How have the two writers described the scenes, places and characters they are writing about? For each poem you should write about:

* the details of the scene
* the feelings of the people
* the poet's use of language.

 Remember to support your answer with examples from each text.

1Ag. 'WHEREVER I HANG' BY GRACE NICHOLS

Essay Preparation

In pairs, discuss and make brief notes in response to the following questions.

VERSE 1:

1 What does she miss/not miss about moving to England from her homeland?
2 Does the use of her own language make her feelings more easily understood?
3 How does she describe her new 'self' and what does she mean?
4 Why is the simile 'people pouring from the underground system/like beans' an effective one?
5 How does she emphasise her anxiety as to whether things are real (true), or not real (false)?

VERSE 2:

6 Gradually, she says, she changes her 'calypso ways'. What do you think she means by this? Do you think it is an effective description?
7 What does she do that shows she is learning to fit into the English way of life?
8 What is her basic problem?

VERSE 3:

9 To what oceans does the phrase 'divided to de ocean' refer?
10 The last line is delightfully light-hearted – perhaps showing that her willingness and ability to adapt is through her sense of humour. What do you think?

 EXAM PRACTICE ESSAYS

Essay

Compare 'Wherever I Hang' with 'Where the Scattering Began' by Merle Collins in which the subject is similar but the situation is very different. How do the two poets describe the events and characters in their poems? Which poem do you think is the most effective?

 Remember to support your answer with examples from the texts.

Foundation Tier Essay

Compare 'Wherever I Hang' with *one* other poem in **Collection A: In Such a Time as This** that shows the strength of a person's feelings.
For each poem you should write about:

* the description of the situation
* the characters' feelings and attitudes
* the poet's use of language.

 Remember to support your answer with examples from each text.

1Ah. 'WHERE THE SCATTERING BEGAN' BY MERLE COLLINS

Essay Preparation

In pairs, discuss and make brief notes in response to the following questions.

1. The poet uses the word 'Here' to start her poem and also at the end of line 22. What effect does this have?

2. What does the poet mean when she says:
   > 'we come to find our faces again . . .
   > We come with faces denying names
   > gone English, Irish, Scottish'?

3. What are the people doing when the poet says:
   > 'we come to measure the rhythm of our paces
   > against the call of the Ghanaian drum that talks'?

4. What does the poet mean by:
   > 'We come with hands that speak
   > in the ways the tongue has forgotten'?

5. How do they reshape languages?

6. What 'memory' do they have of a place they have never been?

7. What are the people 'yearning' for when they look at the sky?

8. What might be the 'forest sounds' that they've never known?

9. Do you think that it matters to meet people of your own race and background? Even if you have never lived anywhere else but Britain?

10. What do you think the title 'Where the Scattering Began' means?

 EXAM PRACTICE ESSAYS

Essay

Look again at 'Where the Scattering Began' and 'Refugee Blues' by W.H. Auden, a poem from the **War and Death** section of **Collection A: In a Time Such as This**. How do the two poets describe the situation and feelings of their characters? Which poem do you think is the most effective?

 Remember to support your answer with examples from the texts.

Foundation Tier Essay

Look again at 'Where the Scattering Began' and at *one* other poem in the **New Beginnings** section of **Collection A: In a Time Such as This**. How do the writers of the two poems help you to understand the events or incidents they describe?
For each poem you should write about:

* the details of the scene
* the feelings of the people
* the poet's use of language.

 Remember to support your answer with examples from each text.

19

1Ai. 'THE DARKLING THRUSH' BY THOMAS HARDY

Essay Preparation

In pairs, discuss and make brief notes in response to the following questions.

1   What do you think the title of this poem means?
2   When the poet mentions the 'Winter's dregs', what does he mean?
3   What is the 'eye of day'? Why is it 'weakening'?
4   What two words in lines 5–6 are to do with music? What do they tell us about the shape of the 'bine-stems'?
5   Why is the land described as the 'Century's corpse'?
6   What is:
    a) The 'crypt' of the corpse?
    b) the 'death-lament' of the corpse?
7   What does the poet mean by:
    'The ancient pulse of germ and birth
    Was shrunken hard and dry'?
8   What words does the poet use to describe the thrush? What expectations does this raise? Would you expect him to be full of 'Hope' and 'ecstatic sound'?
9   How does Hardy contrast the bleak countryside with the wonderful song of the bird?
10 Why is Hope written with a capital H? What other words are connected to 'Hope'?

EXAM PRACTICE ESSAYS

Essay

This poem vividly describes the atmosphere and scene. Compare it with 'Dulce et Decorum Est' by Wilfred Owen, a poem in the **War and Death** section of **Collection A: In Such a Time as This** where the atmosphere and scene also are memorable.

 Remember to support your answer with examples from the texts.

Foundation Tier Essay

Look again at 'The Darkling Thrush' and *one* other poem in **Collection A: In Such a Time as This**.
For each poem you should write about:

*   the description of events
*   the characters' feelings and attitudes
*   the poet's use of language.

 Remember to support your answer with examples from each text.

1Aj. 'ELECTRICITY COMES TO COCOA BOTTOM' BY MARCIA DOUGLAS

Essay Preparation

In pairs, discuss and make brief notes in response to the following questions.

VERSE 1: THE 'BUILD-UP'

1 We learn that the children had 'camped' with 'their lamps filled with oil'. What does this tell us?

2 Why do you think Grannie Patterson 'peeped through the crack'? Why didn't she open the door and look out?

3 Put the following phrase into non-poetic language:
'A breeze coming home from the sea held its breath;'.

VERSE 2: THE LIGHTS GO ON!

4 Why is Mr Samuel seen as a 'silhouette'?

5 What is the reaction of the humans? Write down the verb that was used.

6 What are the reactions of the natural world? Write down the verbs that were used.

7 But what had been forgotten?

VERSE 3: WHAT HAD NOT HAPPENED

8 Where had the children gone?

9 Why was it 'too late'?

10 Did it matter that no one recorded the moment?

EXAM PRACTICE ESSAYS

Essay

Look again at 'Electricity Comes to Cocoa Bottom' and at 'The Darkling Thrush' by Thomas Hardy. How do the poets show the feelings and attitudes of the characters involved as night approaches?

 Remember to support your answer with examples from the texts.

Foundation Tier Essay

Look again at 'Electricity Comes to Cocoa Bottom' and 'Hide and Seek' by Vernon Scannell, another poem where the ending was not as expected. Consider in both cases how the poet brings the events and characters to life.

For each poem you should write about:

* the description of events
* the characters' feelings and attitudes
* the poet's use of language.

 Remember to support your answer with examples from each text.

1Ak. 'YOU WILL BE HEARING FROM US SHORTLY' BY U.A. FANTHORPE

Essay Preparation

In pairs, discuss and make brief notes in response to the following questions.

1 What words in the second verse are unpleasant? What pleasant thing is said?

2 How do the interviewers respond to the candidate's answers to their first and second questions?

3 The third question is about age. How do they make it clear that he or she is too old? What was his or her attitude to this?

4 What are the interviewers implying about his or her looks in verse four?

5 What does the enjambment between 'appearance' (line 20) and 'Disturbing?' (line 21) allow for?

6 What do they imply about his or her accent? What do they suggest when their reply to where she was educated is: 'Much of a handicap is that to you,/would you say?'

7 What does the word 'shimmer' suggest about 'domestic disasters'?

8 'And you were born – ?'
'Yes. Pity.' What do you think the feelings of the interviewee would be after such an interview?

9 What is your opinion of the interviewers?

10 Why do you think the poet wrote this poem?

EXAM PRACTICE ESSAYS

Essay

In this poem, as in 'Death in Leamington' by John Betjeman (from the **War and Death** section), the person about whom the poem is written is silent, but in both poems we gain understanding of the person, their life, and/or feelings. Which poem do you think is the most effective, and why?

 Remember to support your answer with examples from the texts.

Foundation Tier Essay

Look again at 'You Will Be Hearing From Us Shortly' and at *one* other poem in the **New Beginnings** section of *Collection A: In Such a Time as This*. Describe the situation the poets are writing about and the feelings of the character(s) involved. For each poem you should write about:

* the description of events
* the characters' feelings and attitudes
* the poet's use of language.

 Remember to support your answer with examples from each text.

1AI.   'REFUGEE BLUES' BY W.H. AUDEN

Essay Preparation

In pairs, discuss and make brief notes in response to the following questions.

1. What two things does the poet mean by saying that the refugees had thought their country 'fair'?
2. In the fourth and fifth verses the consul and the committee both say things that do not make sense – what are they?
3. What is ironic about the speaker saying '... they will steal our daily bread'?
4. What does the poet mean by 'thunder rumbling' in the seventh verse? What is the poetic effect of these words?
5. How does the poet describe how much more fortunate the following are than refugees?
    * domesticated animals
    * fish and birds.
6. Do you think that people are often kinder to animals than people? If so, why?
7. Why are birds able to sing at 'ease'?
8. What difference can politicians make to human lives?
9. Why do you think the poet starts lines with 'Saw', 'Walked', 'Dreamed', and so on instead of 'I saw', 'I walked', 'I dreamed'? What is the effect of this?
10. The last two verses are full of despair with the repetition of 'thousand'. Put the meaning of these verses into your own words.

EXAM PRACTICE ESSAYS

Essay

'Refugee Blues' is a poem about rejection, as is 'You Will Be Hearing From Us Shortly' by U.A. Fanthorpe. Both are about painful experiences. Compare the ways in which the poets have described the events. Which poem do you find the most effective?

 Remember to support your answer with examples from the texts.

Foundation Tier Essay

Look again at 'Refugee Blues' and *one* other poem from **Collection A: In Such a Time as This** in which the poet feels sympathy for the character(s) whose problems he/she is describing.

For each poem you should write about:

* the description of events
* the characters' feelings and attitudes
* the poet's use of language.

 Remember to support your answer with examples from each text.

'WAR MUSIC' BY CHRISTOPHER LOGUE

Essay Preparation

In pairs, discuss and make brief notes in response to the following questions.

1 In a hand-to-hand battle what do you think you would be trying to do? Would you be trying to kill your opponent or make sure that he could not kill you?

2 What does the word 'tickered' tell you about the arrows?

3 What was Prince Hector's main aim in this battle? How does the poet stress this?

4 What does the poet mean when he says that before his fight with Ajax, Hector was 'pulling the Trojans out a yard or two'?

5 What do we usually use the word 'bait' in connection with? How would Hector 'bait' Ajax with his throat?

6 What does the poet mean when he says, 'and Ajax took'?

7 Which two words in lines 20–21 tell us that Hector found it easy to destroy Ajax's spear?

8 What does the poet mean when he calls both Ajax and the spear 'empty topped'?

9 Which three words are repeated twice in lines 24–25 to emphasise Ajax's slow response?

10 What finally makes Ajax decide to admit defeat?

 EXAM PRACTICE ESSAYS

Essay

'War Music' gives a heroic description of war. Compare it to the realistic description of war in 'Dulce et Decorum Est' by Wilfred Owen. Which description of war do you find most effective?

 Remember to support with examples from the texts.

Foundation Tier Essay

'War Music' gives a particularly vivid description of the scene and the two characters involved. Look at *one* other poem from **Collection A: In Such a Time as This** in which the situation and/or characters are described in detail, and compare the two poems.

For each poem you should write about:

* the description of events
* the characters' feelings and attitudes
* the poet's use of language.

 Remember to support your answer with examples from each text.

1An. 'THE SEND-OFF' BY WILFRED OWEN

Essay Preparation

In pairs, discuss and make brief notes in response to the following questions.

1 What time of day were the men sent off to war?

2 Why do you think they were sent away at that time of day?

3 Who was there to see them leave in the train?

4 What do you think the poet's purpose is in using personification in this poem?

5 What does the simile 'like wrongs hushed-up' tell us? What does the poet think is 'wrong' about their leaving? Why were they being 'hushed-up'?

6 What do you think is the meaning of lines 14–15?
　'Nor there if they yet mock what women meant
　Who gave them flowers.'

7 What does the poet mean by 'beatings of great bells'?

8 What would be the attitude of the soldiers who eventually returned home?

9 Why would the soldiers' return home *not* be an occasion for rejoicing?

10 Find two examples of alliteration in this poem and say what it adds.

 EXAM PRACTICE ESSAYS

Essay

'The Send-off' is an evocative description of the atmosphere surrounding the departure of the soldiers. Compare it with 'The Darkling Thrush' by Thomas Hardy, another poem in which the setting and atmosphere are memorable.

 Remember to support your answer with examples from the texts.

Foundation Tier Essay

Look again at 'The Send-off' and at *one* other poem from **Collection A: In Such a Time as This**, saying how the poets have described the situation and the feelings of the characters.

For each poem you should write about:

✱ the way in which the poet describes the scene and the atmosphere
✱ the characters' feelings and attitudes
✱ the poet's use of language.

 Remember to support your answer with examples from each text.

25

1Ao.

'DULCE ET DECORUM EST' BY WILFRED OWEN

Essay Preparation

In pairs, discuss and make brief notes in response to the following quetions.

1 What does the word 'sludge' tell you about the conditions the soldiers had to endure?
2 What does 'blood-shod' mean?
3 What was the condition of the soldiers after their time in the trenches? How were they feeling? What was the state of their clothes? Write down four words from lines 6–7 which the poet uses to describe the state of the men.
4 The first two lines of the second verse are written in the present tense. Why do you think the poet does this?
5 What are the men 'just in time' for?
6 Write down the two similes describing the effect of gas on the man who failed to put his gas mask on. Describe how these similes tell us what happened to the man, and why they are so effective.
7 What does Owen mean when he says:
    'Dim through the misty panes and thick green light,
    As under a green sea, I saw him drowning'?
8 How can one tell from the third and fourth verses that the man's death was a long drawn out and painful one?
9 Why does Owen start the fourth verse with 'If' and repeat 'If' at line 21?
10 Wilfred Owen felt strongly that in the past, war was only described as 'heroic' and that the reality needed to be told. Do you think he was right?

EXAM PRACTICE ESSAYS

Essay

'Dulce et Decorum Est' describes the atmosphere and scene vividly. Look too, at the other poem in the **War and Death** section by Wilfred Owen, 'The Send-off' which also clearly describes the atmosphere and scene. How effective do you think these two poems are in describing the reality of war?

 Remember to support your answer with examples from the texts.

Foundation Tier Essay

Look again at 'Dulce et Decorum Est' and *one* other poem from **Collection A: In Such a Time as This**. How do the poets describe the events and characters they are writing about? For each poem you should write about:

* the description of the scene and atmosphere
* the feelings and condition of the characters involved
* the poet's use of language.

 Remember to support your answer with examples from each text.

26

'DEATH IN LEAMINGTON' BY JOHN BETJEMAN

Essay Preparation

In pairs, discuss and make brief notes in response to the following questions.

1 What does the poet mean by saying her 'fingers ... Were as dead as the spoken word'?
2 What were the actions of the nurse when she came into the room? Why did the nurse speak in a 'tiny' voice?
3 What kind of house is it? Look up 'stucco' and 'Italianate' to check their meanings.
4 What state was the house in? Which words tell us?
5 What is a 'mantle'?
6 Which decade of the twentieth century do you think the death took place in? What words or facts make you think this?
7 What does the poet mean by 'Chintzy, chintzy cheeriness'?
8 What word does 'silent' in line 25 relate to alliteratively in the second verse?
9 Can you describe what the poet meant when he wrote:
'As the calm of a Leamington ev'ning
Drifted into the place.'
10 What are the nurse's actions in the last verse and why does she do this?

EXAM PRACTICE ESSAYS

Essay

The atmosphere in this poem is calm, yet clearly expressed by the poet. Look at 'Electricity Comes to Cocoa Bottom' by Marcia Douglas where the atmosphere is also clearly recreated. Which poem do you find the most effective?

 Remember to support your answer with examples from the texts.

Foundation Tier Essay

Look again at 'Death in Leamington' and *one* other poem from **Collection A: In Such a Time as This**. How do the two poets recreate the scenes and atmosphere they are describing?

For each poem you should write about:

∗ the description of the setting and events
∗ the atmosphere that pervades the poem
∗ the poet's use of language.

 Remember to support your answer with examples from each text.

Collection B: Identity

You will need to teach all the poems in *Collection B: Identity*, although for the questions in both the English and English Literature examinations students will be focusing on just two (or three) poems from one of the collections. The questions will obviously be concerned with the theme of *Identity* and will require them to write lengthily and exploratively about:

* The content of the poems: their meanings, themes, the message each poet is trying to put over to the reader.

* The language of the poems: the words, phrases, sentences and images each poet uses.

* The presentation of the poems: how they are set out, what kind of verse patterns they have, their rhyme and rhythm, and so on.

For the English Literature examination they will have to make comparisons between the poems. In order to do this they will need to see clearly the features the poems have in common and be able to make cross-references.

All of these considerations have been dealt with in the Student's Book – and the work in this Teacher's Resource has been designed to complement it.

1Ba. 'WARNING' BY JENNY JOSEPH

Essay Preparation

In pairs, discuss and make brief notes in response to the following questions.

1 List the main examples of 'growing old disgracefully' that the poet considers in the first verse.

2 What does the poet mean by 'the sobriety of my youth' (line 8)?

3 Why is line 11 so short?

4 What effect do the three 'ands' have in line 15 of the second verse?

5 How does the tone of the poem change in the third verse?

6 What is the purpose of the rhetorical question in the last verse?

7 Comment on the importance of tenses and pronouns in this poem.

8 What does the poet's attitude to **a)** freedom, **b)** responsibility, seem to be?

9 Were you shocked or surprised at anything in this poem? Explain why or why not.

10 What is the significance of the title?

 EXAM PRACTICE ESSAYS

Essay

Compare 'Warning' with *one* other poem, in the **Old Age** section of **Collection B: Identity**, for example, 'Old Man, Old Man', 'Follower' or 'Mirror'.

Explore in detail the different attitudes to old age in the two poems.

 Remember to support your answer with examples from the texts.

Foundation Tier Essay

Look again at 'Warning' by Jenny Joseph and 'Once Upon a Time' by Gabriel Okara. How do they convey their different attitudes towards old age?

For each poem you should write about:

* the poet's feelings about aging
* their attitudes to others
* the poet's use of language.

 Remember to support your answer with examples from each text.

1Bb.   'MIRROR' BY SYLVIA PLATH

Essay Preparation

In pairs, discuss and make brief notes in response to the following questions.

1. Pick out from the poem the other words or phrases which show that the mirror is 'exact' (line 1) in what it sees.

2. Why do you think Plath describes the mirror as 'a little god'?

3. What does the mirror seem to think about the wall opposite? Pick out words or phrases to support your answer.

4. Which two things separate the mirror from the wall?

5. In what sense is the mirror like 'a lake'? Which words or ideas in the second verse add to this effect?

6. Why does Plath describe candles and the moon as 'those liars'?

7. Pick out a simile in the second verse and explain what it adds to the poem.

8. Try to put the last two lines of the poem into your own words.

9. Look up the words: 'preconceptions', 'meditate', and 'agitation' and write down their meanings.

10. What impression does the whole poem give about the woman's attitude to aging?

EXAM PRACTICE ESSAYS

Essay

Both 'Mirror' and 'Warning' are written by women. How far do you think they show particularly feminine views of old age? Do you think men feel the same or differently about it?

 Remember to support your answer with examples from the texts.

Foundation Tier Essay

Look again at 'Mirror' and 'Warning' by Jenny Joseph. Show how their views of old age differ. You should write about:

* why the woman in 'Mirror' dreads old age
* why the woman in 'Warning' looks forward to it
* how the poets use vivid language to express their ideas.

 Remember to support your answer with examples from the texts.

30

1Bc.

'OLD MAN, OLD MAN' BY U.A. FANTHORPE

Essay Preparation

In pairs, discuss and make brief notes in response to the following questions.

1 Pick out some of the adjectives and verbs which the poet uses to describe her father (for example, 'shamble', 'obdurate'). What do they add to the poem?

2 Using the evidence in the poem, decide what kind of a father and husband the 'Old Man' has been. Pick out words or phrases to support your points.

3 What particular talents did he have when he was younger?

4 What do the words 'Lord', 'World authority' and 'connoisseur' suggest that his daughter thinks about the old man's character?

5 What do the phrases 'timetabled cigarette' and 'Self-demoted ... to washing-up', tell us about the old man's present way of life?

6 From what he says (in italics) and how he behaves on his daughter's visit, what does he seem to feel?

7 Look up the words: 'recalcitrant', 'obdurate', 'surliness', and 'disinherited'. Why do you think the poet chose this particular vocabulary?

8 Why does the poet say her father lives in a 'contracted world'?

9 What do the last two lines suggest about the daughter's emotional response to her father?

10 What does the phrase 'your wife' rather than 'my mother' suggest?

EXAM PRACTICE ESSAYS

Essay

Examine the reversals of power in 'Old Man, Old Man' and either 'Follower' by Seamus Heaney or 'Once Upon a Time' by Gabriel Okara.

 Remember to support your answer with examples from the texts.

Foundation Tier Essay

Look again at 'Old Man, Old Man' and 'Miracle on St David's Day' by Gillian Clarke. Compare the portrayal of the 'Old Man' with that of the 'big, mild man'.

You should write about:

* the life lived by both men
* their behaviour on the 'day' of each poem
* the way the poets describe them.

 Remember to support your answer with examples from the texts.

31

1Bd.   **'FOLLOWER' BY SEAMUS HEANEY**

Essay Preparation

In pairs, discuss and make brief notes in response to the following questions.

1   Pick out the things the son admired about his father in the first three verses.

2   Find one simile in those verses: explain its meaning and say how effective you find it.

3   Look at the use of active verbs in this poem (for example, the horses 'strained', the sod 'rolled'). Underline any examples you can see in each verse.

4   How do these active verbs add to your understanding of the poem?

5   What does it mean to follow in someone's shadow?

6   When did the poet stop doing this?

7   Why are the sods of earth described as 'polished'?

8   The main contrast in the poem is summed up in the last verse. What is it?

9   Why is the title doubly important in this poem?

10   Who is the most patient in this poem? Justify your answer with examples from the text.

 EXAM PRACTICE ESSAYS

Essay

Compare the attitudes of the adult children to their aged parents in 'Follower' and 'Old Man, Old Man' by U.A. Fanthorpe. Refer to both the ideas in the poems and the language used by the poets.

 Remember to support your answer with examples from the texts.

Foundation Tier Essay

Look again at 'Follower' and 'Once Upon a Time' by Gabriel Okara. How do the two poets show the relationships between the fathers and their sons?

You should write about:

✱ the relationship as shown in 'Follower'
✱ the relationship as shown in 'Once Upon a Time'
✱ the poets' use of language.

 Remember to support your answer with examples from the texts.

1Be. 'AT GRASS' BY PHILIP LARKIN

Essay Preparation

In pairs, discuss and make brief notes in response to the following questions.

1   Explain 'distresses' and 'anonymous' as used in the first verse.

2   How does the poet build up a picture of 'classic Junes' in the second and third verses?

3   Explain the meaning of the last two and a half lines in the third verse.

4   Why is the simile at the beginning of the fourth verse particularly appropriate?

5   What kind of question does line 19 contain? What does the 'answer' seem to be?

6   Why is the horses' present home called 'the unmolesting meadows'?

7   What ideas are linked together in '. . . they/Have slipped their names, and stand at ease'?

8   Why must the horses' present galloping be for 'joy'?

9   Do they seem to miss the 'fieldglass' and 'stop-watch'? Give reasons for your answer.

10   How long have they been 'At Grass'?

EXAM PRACTICE ESSAYS

Essay

Compare the old age of the horses in 'At Grass' to the portrayal of old age in humans in one or two other poems from the **Old Age** section of **Collection B: Identity**.

Remember to support your answer with examples from the texts.

Foundation Tier Essay

Look again at 'At Grass' and 'Old Man, Old Man' by U.A. Fanthorpe. Compare the different ways that old age is shown in the two poems.

You should write about:

* the past life of the old horses and the old man
* their present lives
* the poets' use of language.

Remember to support your answer with examples from the texts.

33

1Bf. 'I SHALL PAINT MY NAILS RED' BY CAROLE SATYAMURTI

Essay Preparation

In pairs, discuss and make brief notes in response to the following questions.

1 Why does the poet use the indefinite 'I Shall' instead of the more definite 'I Will'?

2 What does she mean by '... a bit of colour is a public service'?

3 Why does she think she 'will look like a survivor' if she paints her nails red?

4 How does she expect her daughter and her lover to react?

5 What impression do you think she wants to make on them?

6 What does she mean by 'a ten-minute moratorium'?

7 What indication is there that she is not really wanting to make a permanent change to her appearance?

8 Why does she choose not to dye her hair red?

9 Would that gesture (of dyeing her hair) have made more impact?

10 What impressions have you formed of the poet's character from what she has written? Refer to the poem in detail in your answer.

EXAM PRACTICE ESSAYS

Essay

Look again at 'I Shall Paint my Nails Red' and compare it with 'Warning' by Jenny Joseph and 'Still I Rise' by Maya Angelou. What do the three poems have in common and how do they differ? Refer in detail to the poets' ideas and the language they use.

 Remember to support your answer with examples from the texts.

Foundation Tier Essay

Look again at 'I Shall Paint my Nails Red' and 'Still I Rise' by Maya Angelou. Compare how the two poets express their self-confidence.
For each poem you write about:

* the content of the poem
* how the poets express their self-confidence
* the poets' use of language.

 Remember to support your answer with examples from each text.

1Bg. 'ONCE UPON A TIME' BY GABRIEL OKARA

Essay Preparation

In pairs, discuss and make brief notes in response to the following questions.

1 Explain in your own words, the difference between people laughing 'with their hearts' and 'with their teeth'.

2 Why do you think the poet refers to their 'ice-block cold eyes' instead of their 'ice-cold eyes'?

3 Pick out two of the contrasts the poet makes in the first three verses between 'once upon a time' and 'now'. What is the point he is trying to make?

4 Select three to four of the main things the poet says he has 'learned' in the fourth and fifth verses.

5 Do you think it is possible or indeed desirable to always be honest in social situations? Give reasons for your answer.

6 What do you think the poet means when he says to his son, 'I want to be what I used to be/when I was like you'?

7 What does he mean by 'muting' things?

8 What is the difference between 'unlearn' and 'relearn'?

9 Pick out two similes from the poem and comment on what they add to the poem.

10 Is this poem completely serious, or is there a funny side to it? Refer in detail to the poem in your answer.

EXAM PRACTICE ESSAYS

Essay

Consider how the poets in 'Once Upon a Time' and 'Still I Rise' explore the meanings of freedom in their poems.

 Remember to support your answer with examples from the texts.

Foundation Tier Essay

Look again at 'Once Upon a Time' and 'Follower' by Seamus Heaney. How do they deal with the changes that age brings?

For each poem you should write about:

* the apparent changes due to aging
* the poets' attitudes to these
* the poets' use of language.

 Remember to support your answer with examples from each text.

35

1Bh. 'DEATH OF A NATURALIST' BY SEAMUS HEANEY

Essay Preparation

1 What do the verbs 'festered', 'rotted', 'sweltered', and 'gargled' add to the first ten lines of the poem?
2 Pick out a metaphor and a simile in the first ten lines and comment on their effectiveness.
3 Why do you think the poet says 'But best of all' before describing the frogspawn?
4 Why did he fill jampots with frogspawn every spring?
5 Pick out two descriptions of the frogspawn between lines 11–21 and say what they reveal about the poet's attitude to it.
6 Explain, in your own words, what happened 'one hot day' in lines 22–23 to change the poet's view of frogs forever.
7 Pick out three phrases describing the frogs in the last verse which show the poet's changing feelings about them.
8 Pick out two similes in the last verse and say what they add to the sense of 'obscene threat' perceived by the poet.
9 Pick out three 'sound' words (two of them examples of onomatopoeia) in the last five lines of the poem and explain what effect they produce.
10 What 'vengeance' did the poet expect?

EXAM PRACTICE ESSAYS

Essay

Look again at 'Death of a Naturalist' and 'Mid-Term Break', also by Seamus Heaney. Compare how the strength of feeling is built up in each poem. Say which you prefer and why.

 Remember to support your answer with examples from the texts.

Foundation Tier Essay

Look again at 'Death of a Naturalist' and 'The Barn', also by Seamus Heaney. How does the poet show the two different experiences of fear in childhood?

For each poem you should write about:

* the nature of the fear
* how the fear is built up
* the poet's use of language.

 Remember to support your answer with examples from each text.

1Bi. 'THE ROAD NOT TAKEN' BY ROBERT FROST

Essay Preparation

1 What is the time of day and season of the year in this poem?

2 In what ways were the roads different? In what ways were the roads the same?

3 How did the traveller make his decision? What decision would you have made if you had been in his place? Why?

4 Explain 'and wanted wear' in line 8.

5 Explain, in your own words, the last two lines of the third verse.

6 Examine the role of symbolism in the poem.

7 What does the poet appear to feel about the decision that was made?

8 Why do you think the poet repeats 'I' in lines 3 and 4 of the last verse?

9 Why has the poet called the poem 'The Road Not Taken' rather than 'The Road Taken'?

10 What does the word 'diverged' mean and why does the poet repeat the line in which it occurs?

EXAM PRACTICE ESSAYS

Essay

Look again at 'The Road Not Taken' and *one* other poem in **Collection B: Identity** where the poet takes a positive view of his or her own actions. Consider how the two poets explore freedom of choice in their poems.

 Remember to support your answer with examples from the texts.

Foundation Tier Essay

Look again at 'The Road Not Taken' and one other poem of your choice from **Collection B: Identity**, which deals with some kind of decision-making.

For each poem you should write about:

✱ how the poet made their choice
✱ what they felt about this (then and/or later)
✱ the poet's use of language.

 Remember to support your answer with examples from each text.

1Bj. 'MID-TERM BREAK' BY SEAMUS HEANEY

Essay Preparation

1   What impression is given about the poet in the first verse?

2   However, what does the clue of 'bells knelling' link up with in the second verse?

3   How does the poet seem to get on with his youngest sibling?

4   What embarrasses the poet when he arrives home?

5   What is the poet's position in the family and how is this revealed in the poem?

6   Explain, with close reference to the poem, his father's and mother's different reactions to his brother's death.

7   What is meant by 'Snowdrops/And candles soothed the bedside'?

8   How old was his brother and what exactly had happened to him?

9   Why is the 'bruise' likened to a poppy and what do poppies suggest?

10   How upset do you think the poet is by the loss of his brother? Refer closely to the poem to support your answer.

EXAM PRACTICE ESSAYS

Essay

Look again at 'Mid-Term Break' and either 'Warning' by Jenny Joseph or 'Miracle on St David's Day' by Gillian Clarke. Examine how the poets use the element of surprise in their poems.

Remember to support your answer with examples from the texts.

Foundation Tier Essay

Look again at 'Mid-Term Break' and 'Miracle on St David's Day' by Gillian Clarke. How do both poems use the element of surprise to advantage?

For each poem you should write about:

*   the nature of the 'surprise'
*   how it is built up and finally revealed
*   how the language helps to convey surprise.

Remember to support your answer with examples from each text.

1Bk. 'MIRACLE ON ST DAVID'S DAY' BY GILLIAN CLARKE

Essay Preparation

1 What does the poet mean by describing the afternoon as 'open-mouthed/with daffodils'?

2 Why does line 6 come as a shock after the first five lines? Which two words in the first verse *hint* at all not being as it seems?

3 Write brief notes on the four patients referred to in the second, third and fourth verses.

4 What did the poet feel, and why, at the beginning of the fifth verse?

5 How does she describe the labourer's voice in the fourth and fifth verses?

6 How do the nurses and patients react to the new sound? What effect does his recitation seem to have on the daffodils themselves?

7 What do you think the poet might be suggesting by the last line of the poem?

8 What exactly is the 'miracle' and why does the poet note that it is St David's Day (1 March)?

9 Describe the poet's attitude to the patients. How do they appear to be treated? Pick out particular words to support your points.

10 What do you think might happen next in the life of the 'miracle' man?

EXAM PRACTICE ESSAYS

Essay

Look again at 'Miracle on St David's Day' and *one* other poem of your choice from **Collection B: Identity** which also deals with the subject of change. Comment on how the poets develop the idea of change and convey its outcomes.

 Remember to support your answer with examples from the texts.

Foundation Tier Essay

Look again at 'Miracle on St David's Day' and 'Still I Rise' by Maya Angelou. Write about how each poet has helped you to understand:

✱ the characters' feelings
✱ the events described.

 Remember to support your answer with examples from each text.

39

1Bl. **'THE BARN' BY SEAMUS HEANEY**

Essay Preparation

1 Look at the simile in line 1. Which two senses are closely linked in it? Explain how.

2 What impression is given of the pile of corn in line 2?

3 Why is 'hoarded' a particularly good verb in line 3?

4 How is 'armoury' linked to the third verse?

5 Describe briefly, *in your own words*, the inside of the barn. Use the information from the first, second and third verses to help you.

6 Why does the poet use alliteration in line 12?

7 What emotion is suggested by 'scuttled fast' in line 13?

8 Which three animals seemed to terrify the boy in his sleep?

9 How does he seem to imagine himself in the last verse? Pick out supporting evidence from the poem.

10 There are a number of vivid similes in this poem. Pick out any two and say *why* you think they are successful and *what* they add to the poem.

 EXAM PRACTICE ESSAYS

Essay

Look again at the five poems by Seamus Heaney included in the *Edexcel Anthology for GCSE English*. Explain how the poet conveys the experience of childhood trauma in 'The Barn' and *one* other poem.

 Remember to support your answer with examples from the texts.

Foundation Tier Essay

Look again at 'The Barn' and 'Death of a Naturalist' both by Seamus Heaney. Write about how each poem conveys childhood fears.

For each poem you should write about:

* the nature of the fear
* how the poet makes it dramatic
* the poet's use of language.

 Remember to support you answer with examples from each text.

'AN UNKNOWN GIRL' BY MONIZA ALVI

Essay Preparation

1 Explain briefly, in your own words, what happens in the poem.

2 What is the place, time and year in the poem?

3 Describe the hennaing drawn on the poet's palm. Pick out words or phrases from the poem to support your answer.

4 What does the poet mean by 'She is icing my hand'? What does it suggest?

5 Pick out the lines which are repeated two or three times in the poem, then explain why you think the poet has done this.

6 Look at lines 41–42. Pick out and explain three literary devices that the poet has used here.

7 What does the poet seem to feel about 'the unknown girl'?

8 How does the 'peacock' link up with other references to colour in the poem?

9 Why do you think the poem is called 'An Unknown Girl' rather than 'The Peacock' or 'Hennaing'?

10 What do you think the poet's attitude is to 'Western' influences on Indian life?

 EXAM PRACTICE ESSAYS

Essay

Look again at 'An Unknown Girl' and *one* other poem in which colours are important. Explain how the poets incorporate colours into their poems and reveal their importance.

 Remember to support your answer with examples from the texts.

Foundation Tier Essay

Look again at 'An Unknown Girl' and 'Miracle on St David's Day' by Gillian Clarke. Both poems are about very different memorable experiences.

For each poem you should write about:

* how the poets relate their experience
* why they found the experience memorable
* the language the poets use to express their feelings.

 Remember to support your answer with examples from each text.

1Bn. 'NOT MY BEST SIDE' BY U.A. FANTHORPE

Essay Preparation

1 Explain briefly, in your own words, the basic story behind the painting on page 26 of the *Edexcel Anthology for GCSE English*.

2 Why does the 'dragon' say so much about triangles?

3 What does 'ostentatiously beardless' suggest about the dragon's view of St George? How do we know that the girl (in II) shares this view?

4 What does the dragon think of his potential 'victim'?

5 What are the dragon's views about his own death?

6 Which aspects of the dragon does the girl seem to admire? What is so unexpected about her attitudes?

7 St George says that he is 'qualified and equipped to the/Eyebrow.' Pick out words or phrases from III to support this statement.

8 Write down five adjectives which you think best describe the apparent character of St George based on what he says about himself.

9 Which of the three characters do you most prefer, and why? Refer to the poem in detail to support your answer.

10 Can you think of a better title for the poem than the current one?

(EXAM PRACTICE ESSAYS

Essay

Look again at 'Not My Best Side' and *one* of the other poems from the **Individual Experience** section of **Collection B: Identity**. Show how each poet uses multiple viewpoints to advantage.

 Remember to support your answer with examples from the texts.

Foundation Tier Essay

Look again at 'Not My Best Side' and 'Mid-Term Break' by Seamus Heaney. Show how different viewpoints are used to advantage in these poems.

You should write about:

✱ the different viewpoints shown or suggested in each poem
✱ how the viewpoints add meaning or humour
✱ the different language styles used by each poet.

 Remember to support your answer with examples from the texts.

1Bo. 'STILL I RISE' BY MAYA ANGELOU

Essay Preparation

1 What does the poet mean by 'bitter, twisted lies' in the first verse?

2 What does 'sassiness' (line 5) and 'haughtiness' (line 17) mean?

3 What do you think the poet's walk is like in the second verse? (Try to use your own words.)

4 What does she mean by 'I'll rise' and 'I rise'?

5 What three things does she compare herself to in the third verse?

6 Why does she feel that people might want to see her 'broken'?

7 Why does she mention 'oil wells' and 'gold mines'?

8 Why does she compare herself to 'dust' and 'air'?

9 Why do you think the verse-form changes from line 29 to the end?

10 What does she mean by 'history's shame' and 'a black ocean'?

11 Explain what is meant by line 40.

EXAM PRACTICE ESSAYS

Essay

Look again at 'Still I Rise' and 'Digging' by Seamus Heaney. Explain how the two poets view their relationships with their ancestral pasts and how they see their contributions to the present.

 Remember to support your answer with examples from the texts.

Foundation Tier Essay

Look again at 'Still I Rise' and 'The Road Not Taken' by Robert Frost. Both poets view their present partly in terms of their past.

Show how each poet:

* regards the past
* sees the present and future
* uses language to show these views.

 Remember to support your answer with examples from each text.

1Bp. 'DIGGING' BY SEAMUS HEANEY

Essay Preparation

1 What is suggested by the simile in the first verse?

2 What memory of the past is evoked in the second verse?

3 What does the poet admire about his father and his grandfather?

4 What is the tone of the fifth verse?

5 Pick out any phrase or line of description and say what you think it means and why you like it.

6 Pick out a metaphor and a simile from the poem and explain what you think they add to it.

7 What memories 'awaken' in his head in the seventh verse?

8 In what sense can line 28 be seen as the crux or climax of the poem?

9 How does the poet see himself in relation to his ancestors?

10 Comment as fully as possible on the last line of the poem.

EXAM PRACTICE ESSAYS

Essay

Look again at 'Digging' and 'Still I Rise' by Maya Angelou. Show how the two poets see themselves in relation to their ancestors.

 Remember to support your answer with examples from the texts.

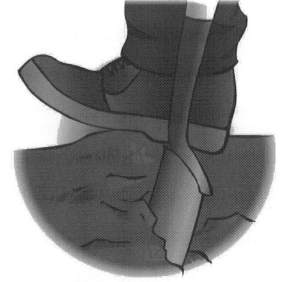

Foundation Tier Essay

Look again at 'Digging' and 'Follower' both by Seamus Heaney. Explain the poet's changing views of his father and himself.

For each poem you should write about:

* how the poem depicts his father
* the poet's changing attitude to him
* the poet's use of language to express his thoughts.

 Remember to support your answer with examples from each text.

(Collection C:) Nature

You need to teach all the poems in the *Collection C: Nature* although for the questions in both the English and English Literature examinations the students will be focusing on just two (or three) poems. The questions will obviously be concerned with the theme of *Nature* and will require them to write lengthily and exploratively about:

* The content of the poems: their meanings, themes, the message each poet is trying to put over to the reader.

* The language of the poems: the words, phrases, sentences and images each poet uses.

* The presentation of the poems: how they are set out, what kind of verse patterns they have, their rhyme and rhythm, and so on.

For the English Literature examination they will have to make comparisons between the poems. In order to do this they will need to see clearly the features the poems have in common and be able to make cross-references.

All of these considerations have been dealt with in the Student's Book – and the work in this Teacher's Resource has been designed to complement it.

1Ca. **'THE HORSES' BY EDWIN MUIR**

Essay Preparation

In pairs, discuss and make brief notes in response to the following questions.

1 What is suggested by 'a twelvemonth' instead of a year?

2 What does a 'covenant with silence' suggest?

3 What image tells us that the war was worldwide?

4 Why do the islanders not want a return to the 'bad old world'?

5 What is suggested by the simile that describes the tractors?

6 Find another simile that describes the arrival of the horses, and comment on its effectiveness.

7 Why were the returning horses strange?

8 Put 'long-lost archaic companionship' in simpler English.

9 Explain the contrast the poet is making in lines 51–52.

10 Comment as fully as possible on the last line.

 EXAM PRACTICE ESSAYS

Essay

Look again at 'The Horses' and 'Roe-Deer' by Ted Hughes. Explain how the two poets see humanity's past and present relationship with these animals.

 Remember to support your answer with examples from the texts, and refer to the poets' use of language.

Foundation Tier Essay

Look again at 'The Horses' and 'The Stag' by Ted Hughes. Write about how each poet has helped you to understand something about the natural world.

For each poem you should write about:

* the events described
* humanity's relationship with these animals
* how the poet has used language to express thought.

 Remember to support your answer with examples from each text.

1Cb. ‘THE THOUGHT-FOX’ BY TED HUGHES

Essay Preparation

In pairs, discuss and make brief notes in response to the following questions.

1 In the first line the poet uses alliteration. Explain why this is effective.

2 Which word would you say sets the mood of the first two verses?

3 Look at the expression in the third verse, ‘Two eyes serve a movement’. Explain what this means and why it is effective. You will need to use your imagination.

4 Why does the poet repeat ‘now’? What is the relationship between the fox’s movements and his own?

5 Explain the double meaning of ‘prints’, ‘stump’ and ‘clearings’.

6 Why does the poet say ‘Coming about its own business’ rather than the more usual ‘Going . . .’?

7 Comment on the effectiveness of the alliteration in line 21.

8 Why does the poet refer to his head as a ‘dark hole’?

9 Why do the last two lines refer to the poem’s beginning? What is the effect of this?

10 Why is the last line shorter than the others?

 EXAM PRACTICE ESSAYS

Essay

Look again at ‘The Thought-Fox’ and ‘A Blade of Grass’ by Brian Patten. Explain how both poets view writing poetry and their relationship with the subject matter.

 Remember to support your answer with examples from the texts.

Foundation Tier Essay

Look again at ‘The Thought-Fox’ and ‘The Trout’ by Seamus Heaney. Comment on how both poets use their imagination to describe the living creatures.

For each poem show how the poet:

* views the creature
* uses language to express his view.

 Remember to support your answer with examples from each text.

47

1Cc. 'THE STAG' BY TED HUGHES

Essay Preparation

In pairs, discuss and make brief notes in response to the following questions.

1 In what sense does the stag have a 'private forest' to run through?

2 Describe the contrast in the second verse between the mood and activity of the people and the stag.

3 Why did the blue horseman behave as he did? Why did he feel 'rather foolish'?

4 Each of the last lines of the first four verses describes the stag using a different verb. Comment on what Hughes suggests in this way.

5 Comment on how Hughes achieves a complete change of mood in the fifth verse.

6 What does the expression 'the camouflage of their terrible planet' suggest? What kind of tone is Hughes using?

7 Comment on the way Hughes conveys the stag's distress and exhaustion in the last verse.

8 Why does the poet repeat the word 'strange' in the last verse?

9 How does the behaviour of the hounds contrast with that of the stag?

10 What is Hughes suggesting in the last two lines about people who go to stag hunts?

EXAM PRACTICE ESSAYS

Essay

Look again at 'The Stag' and 'Roe-Deer', also by Ted Hughes. Explain how the poet views these animals and their relationship with humans.

 Remember to support your answer with examples from the texts.

Foundation Tier Essay

Look again at 'The Stag' and 'Roe-Deer', also by Ted Hughes. Discuss how both poems show the 'secret' and 'private' world of the animals being disturbed by humans.

For each poem you should write about:

* the description of the animals in their natural environment
* the effect of humans on the animals.

 Remember to support your answers with examples from each text.

48

1Cd. 'ROE-DEER' BY TED HUGHES

Essay Preparation

In pairs, discuss and make brief notes in response to the following questions.

1 Comment on the poet's use of 'dimension' in line 3. What is he trying to suggest?

2 What does line 5 tell you about the deer?

3 What does the poet have in mind by 'my snow-screen vision of the abnormal'?

4 Explain ' the all-way disintegration'. Why is it so effective in summing up what was happening?

5 What thought does the poet have in the fifth verse? Explain fully his thought process.

6 Why is the seventh verse unlike all the others?

7 Explain the metaphor 'they rode their legs / Away'. Why is it so effective?

8 Explain the metaphor 'boil of big flakes'. How effective is it?

9 How effective is the last verse as a suitable ending for the poem?

10 'Ordinary' in the last line contrasts with 'abnormal' in line 6. What point is the poet making?

EXAM PRACTICE ESSAYS

Essay

Look again at 'Roe-Deer' and a poem of your choice from **Collection C: Nature**. What attitudes to nature are revealed in the poem?

 Remember to support your answer with examples from the texts.

Foundation Tier Essay

Look again at 'Roe-Deer' and 'Iguana Memory' by Grace Nichols. Both poets have a brief meeting with a living creature.

For each poem show how the poet:

* sees the creature
* learns from the experience
* uses language to show his or her view.

 Remember to support your answer with examples from each text.

49

'BREAK OF DAY IN THE TRENCHES'
BY ISAAC ROSENBERG

Essay Preparation

In pairs, discuss and make brief notes in response to the following questions.

1   Why does the poet capitalise 'Time'?

2   Why does he call time a 'druid'? Who were Druids and what do we associate with them?

3   What does the word 'sardonic' mean? What does it tell us about the rat?

4   What are 'cosmopolitan sympathies'?

5   What does the poet think the rat is mocking and why?

6   What does the expression 'Bonds to the whims of murder' tell you about the poet's own sympathies?

7   The poet questions what the rat sees in the eyes of the soldiers. Is this a rhetorical question?

8   In what sense might the poppies be said to have roots 'in man's veins'?

9   What do the poppies symbolise?

10   What is your overall impression of this poem?

EXAM PRACTICE ESSAYS

Essay

Compare 'Break of Day in the Trenches' with another poem from **Collection C: Nature** which features a poet's encounter with an animal. Which description do you find the most realistic and the most meaningful?

 Remember to support your answer with examples from the texts.

Foundation Tier Essay

Look again at 'Break of Day in the Trenches' and 'Roe-Deer' by Ted Hughes. Describe the situations the two poets are writing about and the feelings involved.

For each poem you should write about:

✱   a description of what takes place
✱   the feelings of humans and animals
✱   the poet's use of language.

 Remember to support your answer with examples from each text.

1Cf. 'WIND' BY TED HUGHES

Essay Preparation

In pairs, discuss and make brief notes in response to the following questions.

1 In what sense has the house 'been far out at sea all night'?

2 Why did the hills have 'new places'?

3 The second verse provides a wonderful description of a wet and windy dawn. Comment on the language Hughes uses to achieve his effect.

4 Explain the metaphor 'The tent of the hills', in the third verse.

5 Comment on the effectiveness of the simile in the fourth verse.

6 In the fifth verse, why does the poet compare his house to a 'fine green goblet'? Explain his use of the image.

7 Describe the mood of the two people in the last two verses.

8 The poet uses personification in the final verse. Identify it and comment on its effectiveness.

9 Make a list of the strong verbs in the poem, and comment on the use Hughes makes of them.

10 How many examples of onomatopoeia can you find in the poem?

EXAM PRACTICE ESSAYS

Essay

Look again at 'Wind' and 'The Storm' by Theodore Roethke. Which poem do you find the most effective in describing the extreme weather? Comment on the ways both poets set the scene and create the atmosphere.

 Remember to support your answer with examples from the texts.

Foundation Tier Essay

Look again at 'Wind' and 'The Storm' by Theodore Roethke. Write about how each poet has helped you to understand:

* the power of the storm
* the different ways people react to it.

 Remember to support your answer with examples from each text.

51

1Cg. 'MUSHROOMS' BY SYLVIA PLATH

Essay Preparation

In pairs, discuss and make brief notes in response to the following questions.

1 Comment on the unusual expression 'very / Whitely'. What is the poet suggesting?

2 What does 'discreetly' mean?

3 What figure of speech is used in the second verse and to what effect?

4 What contrast is made in the fourth verse?

5 In what ways does the poet show the mushrooms' determination?

6 What aspect of a mushroom's character is the poet suggesting in the seventh verse?

7 Why do you think the poet has used repetition in the eighth verse?

8 In line 29 why does the poet say 'in spite'? What effect does it have?

9 What tone might the mushrooms be using to say 'Our kind multiplies'?

10 What do we mean when we speak of someone having 'a foot in the door'? Why is it appropriate here?

EXAM PRACTICE ESSAYS

Essay

Look again at 'Mushrooms' and another poem of your choice from **Collection C: Nature**. Comment on how the two poets convey the power and force of nature.

 Remember to support your answer with examples from each text.

Foundation Tier Essay

Look again at 'Mushrooms' and 'Trout' by Seamus Heaney, two poems which show how living things are naturally equipped to survive.

For each poem show how the poet:

* describes his or her subject
* shows its fitness to survive
* uses language to show his or her view.

 Remember to support your answer with examples from each text.

'THE STORM' BY THEODORE ROETHKE

Essay Preparation

In pairs, discuss and make brief notes in response to the following questions.

1 What is the effect of the alliteration in the first verse?

2 Pick out the examples of onomatopoeia in the first verse. What is their combined effect?

3 Why is the simile in line 15 particularly effective?

4 What does the word 'contending' in line 16 suggest about the wind and the sea?

5 Why, do you imagine, is the door heavy?

6 What indications do we get in lines 18–28 that heavy storms are fairly common occurrences in Santa Lucia?

7 Look up the word 'limber' in a dictionary. How appropriate is its use in line 34?

8 Comment on the mood of the poet and his companions in the third section.

9 Why does the poet bother to describe the spider?

10 Coming after many short sentences and phrases, the last four lines are fairly regular and smooth. What poetic devices does the poet use? What is the effect of the lines?

 EXAM PRACTICE ESSAYS

Essay

'The Storm' gives a vivid description of the scene. Compare it with the realistic description of nature's power in any other poem in **Collection C: Nature** of the *Edexcel Anthology for GCSE English*.

 Remember to support your answer with examples from the texts.

Foundation Tier Essay

Look again at 'The Storm' and 'Break of Day in the Trenches' by Isaac Rosenberg and the way both poets express their thoughts and feelings that danger lies all around.

For each poem you should write about:

∗ a description of the time and place
∗ the poet's attitude to what he sees
∗ the poet's response to the danger.
∗ the poet's use of language.

 Remember to support your answer with examples from each text.

53

1Ci. 'THISTLES' BY TED HUGHES

Essay Preparation

In pairs, discuss and make brief notes in response to the following questions.

1 Comment on the effectiveness of the metaphor in line 2.

2 Why is the example of onomatopoeia in line 3 particularly effective?

3 What can you say about 'a revengeful burst / Of resurrection'?

4 What characteristics of thistles are revealed in the second verse?

5 Why does the poet refer to a 'Viking' in line 7?

6 Explain the pun Hughes is making in the last line of the third verse.

7 How do the thistles compare to men in the last verse?

8 Why does Hughes use the word 'feud'? What is implied by this?

9 Is there any comment on human nature implied in the last line?

10 How do you respond to this poem?

EXAM PRACTICE ESSAYS

Essay

Look again at 'Thistles' and another poem in **Collection C: Nature** of the *Edexcel Anthology for GCSE English* that deals with an aggressive aspect of nature. How do both poets treat their subject and what are their feelings towards it?

 Remember to support your answer with examples from the texts.

Foundation Tier Essay

Look again at 'Thistles' and 'Nettles' by Vernon Scannell. How do the poets react to their subject matter?

For each poem you should write about:

✱ a description of their power to hurt

✱ the way the poet chooses to imagine them

✱ the poet's use of language.

 Remember to support your answer with examples from each text.

1Cj.   'TROUT' BY SEAMUS HEANEY

Essay Preparation

In pairs, discuss and make brief notes in response to the following questions.

1 What is the effect of the metaphor 'Hangs'? How can the trout hang 'deep under' something?

2 Explain the metaphor in the second line of the second verse.

3 How would you describe the mood of the second verse?

4 List the words and expressions that compare the trout to weapons of war, and comment on their effectiveness.

5 Comment on the expression 'cold blood'. What does it tell us about the trout?

6 Why is the last line by itself?

7 Without the title would this be a recognisable description of a trout?

8 There is no mention of humans in this poem – except in the references to man-made weapons. Is Heaney making any point about men?

9 Find an example of alliteration and comment on its effect.

10 Find an example of internal rhyming (i.e. where a rhyme is completed in the middle of a line rather than at the end) and comment on its effect.

EXAM PRACTICE ESSAYS

Essay

'Trout' paints a picture of the fish's bold, fighting qualities. Compare it with any other poem from **Collection C: Nature** that views the subject in a similar way.

 In your answer remember to refer closely to the texts and make references to language.

Foundation Tier Essay

Consider the ways the poets describe nature in 'Trout' and Ted Hughes's 'Thistles'.

For each poem you should write about:

* the way the poet describes their subject matter
* the emotions experienced by the poet and/or reader
* the poet's use of language.

 Remember to support your answer with examples from each text.

1Ck. **'IGUANA MEMORY' BY GRACE NICHOLS**

Essay Preparation

In pairs, discuss and make brief notes in response to the following questions.

1 Comment on the child-like way in which the first verse is expressed.

2 Why is 'green like moving newleaf sunlight' a separate verse?

3 What does the poet achieve by repeating the word 'big'?

4 When the poet says 'so it seemed to me', what is she telling you about her viewpoint?

5 What is so significant about the 'brief / split moment'?

6 The iguana was obviously afraid of the child. What does this tell us about relationships between different species?

7 Comment on the effectiveness of 'for the green of its life'. Why 'green'?

8 Rewrite the poem with punctuation. Comment on the way your version differs in its effect from the original.

9 In what other ways is this poem different from the other poem you have read in the *Edexcel Anthology for GCSE English*?

10 Do you like the poem? Give reasons for your answer.

 (**EXAM PRACTICE ESSAYS**

Essay

Look again at 'Iguana Memory' and another poem from **Collection C: Nature** which is about a brief meeting with a living creature. Compare the ways the poets and the creatures react to each other, and what we learn of nature from this.

 Remember to support your answer with examples from the texts.

Foundation Tier Essay

Look again at 'Iguana Memory' and 'Nettles' by Vernon Scannell, two poems which deal with young children suddenly coming into contact with nature.

For each poem you should write about:

* the importance of the experience
* the characters' feelings
* how natural self-preservation works
* the poets' use of language to show their views.

 Remember to support your answer with examples from each text.

'KEEPING ORCHIDS' BY JACKIE KAY

Essay Preparation

In pairs, discuss and make brief notes in response to the following questions.

1   Explain the striking effect of the first line.

2   Why is the third line a particularly effective simile?

3   Does the poet suggest the crashing of the carafe twice is a matter of coincidence?

4   Explain the symbolism of 'The skin/ shut like an eye in the dark'.

5   Why does the poet seem to need 'the proof of meeting' her mother?

6   What are the words 'Compressed' and 'Airtight' referring to? Why are they separated by full stops?

7   In what sense is it true to say 'A door opens and closes'? What is the poet thinking?

8   What is the point of the poem's title? Explain its significance.

9   What is the poet's attitude to her mother now that she's met her?

10   Has the poet made a decision about anything at the end of the poem?

 EXAM PRACTICE ESSAYS

Essay

Look again at 'Keeping Orchids' and 'The Flowers' by Selima Hill. Both poets use flowers in a symbolic way. Comment on how the poets develop the idea of flowers linking with memories.

 Remember to support your answer with examples from the texts.

Foundation Tier Essay

Look again at 'Keeping Orchids' and 'The Flowers' by Selima Hill, which are both about a poet's feelings for a parent.

For each poem you should write about how the poet has helped you to share:

* her memories
* her sense of loss
* her uncertainty about her relationship with the parent.

 Remember to support your answer with examples from each text.

1Cm. **'NETTLES' BY VERNON SCANNELL**

Essay Preparation

In pairs, discuss and make brief notes in response to the following questions.

1 Comment on the connection between 'green spears' and 'regiment of spite'.

2 How does the poet make us feel sorry for his son?

3 Explain the phrase 'a watery grin'.

4 What does the fact he 'honed the blade' tell us about his anger?

5 Comment on the rhyme scheme of this poem.

6 Find another image that extends the metaphor of fighting.

7 Look up the word 'pyre' in a dictionary. Why does he use it in preference to 'fire'?

8 What might be implied by the word 'fallen'?

9 Do you think the poet has in mind the coming of World War II in the poem? What connection might he be implying between the destruction of the first nettles and the 'tall recruits' that come later?

10 What are your overall impressions of this type of poem which has a regular type of rhyme and rhythm?

EXAM PRACTICE ESSAYS

Essay

Look again at 'Nettles' and another poem from **Collection C: Nature** that describes the force of nature. How do the poets suggest that humans cannot tame nature, but can only learn from it? What do you find most effective?

 Remember to support your answer with examples from the texts.

Foundation Tier Essay

Look again at 'Nettles' and 'Mushrooms' by Sylvia Plath. Compare the ways both poets treat their subject matter.

For each poem you should write about:

* the character of the living thing
* the way it multiplies and survives
* the poet's use of language.

 Remember to support your answer with examples from each text.

1Cn. **'THE FLOWERS' BY SELIMA HILL**

Essay Preparation

In pairs, discuss and make brief notes in response to the following questions.

1. What tone does 'After lunch' set?

2. How do words like 'basket', 'jam-jar' and 'trowel' continue the tone?

3. How does the tone change in the last line of the first verse?

4. What impression of the girl do we form from her actions in the second verse?

5. What impression do we form of the adult from the same verse?

6. What do we make of the poet's hesitation in line 20?

7. What is ironical about the girl's comment *It's finished now*?

8. It would be easy to blame the poet for neglecting her father's grave and to see her being shamed by her daughter's actions. What makes us sense that it is not as simple as that?

9. How does the poet suggest the mood of the two females as they rode home?

10. What does the word 'ruts' symbolise?

 EXAM PRACTICE ESSAYS

Essay

Look again at 'Flowers' and 'A Blade of Grass' by Brian Patten. Discuss the poets' attitudes to the way nature can symbolise deep feelings for us.

 Remember to support your answer with examples from the texts.

Foundation Tier Essay

Look again at 'Flowers' and 'Nettles' by Vernon Scannell. Compare the way both poems involve a parent and a child and the clearing away of weeds.

For each poem you should write about:

* a description of the scene and background
* the feelings and attitudes of the characters involved
* the poet's use of language.

 Remember to support your answer with examples from each text.

1Co. 'THE FIVE STUDENTS' BY THOMAS HARDY

Essay Preparation

In pairs, discuss and make brief notes in response to the following questions.

1   What is the mood of the first verse?

2   Find evidence that the verses stand for the seasons of the year.

3   Why are they described as 'on our urgent way' in the second verse?

4   What does 'briar-meshed plantations' suggest about their life?

5   What is the effect of the word 'fallen' in line 18? Why is it particularly appropriate?

6   Comment on the imagery of the fourth verse. What is it symbolic of?

7   Comment on the imagery of the fifth verse. What does it symbolise?

8   What is the mood of the poet as he lives on?

9   Comment on the use of the word 'stalk'.

10   Why does the poem end with the word 'anon'?

EXAM PRACTICE ESSAYS

Essay

Look again at 'The Five Students' and 'Keeping Orchids' by Jackie Kay. How do the two poets describe their own situation and feelings? Comment on their use of symbols and state which poem you find the most effective.

 Remember to support your answer with examples from the texts.

Foundation Tier Essay

Look again at 'The Five Students' and 'The Flowers' by Selima Hill. How do both poets use nature to show attitudes to the death of others?

For each poem you should write about:

*   a description of the context
*   feelings and emotions expressed
*   the poet's use of language.

 Remember to support your answer with examples from each text.

1Cp. **'A BLADE OF GRASS' BY BRIAN PATTEN**

Essay Preparation

In pairs, discuss and make brief notes in response to the following questions.

1 What is the effect of the first and fourth lines being the same?

2 What appears to be the poet's attitude in line 5?

3 Does the 'frost' simply make the blade of grass prettier?

4 What is the effect of the word 'quite' in line 11?

5 Is the girl right to be indignant?

6 What does the poet think is the 'tragedy', and why?

7 What does this poem mean?

8 Do you agree that the simplicity of the poem is its strength?

9 Do you notice any metaphors or similes in the poem?

10 What is the overall tone of the poem?

 EXAM PRACTICE ESSAYS

Essay

Look at 'A Blade of Grass' and a poem of your choice from **Collection C: Nature**. Discuss how the poets' choice of words conveys the strength of their feelings. Which poem do you prefer, and why?

 Remember to support your answer with examples from the texts.

Foundation Tier Essay

'A Blade of Grass' is making a statement about nature. Look also at another poem from **Collection C: Nature** which makes a statement.

For each poem you should write about:

∗ a discussion of the context or background
∗ what the poet reveals of feelings
∗ the point the poem is making about nature
∗ the poet's use of language.

 Remember to support your answer with examples from each text.

61

2 Non-fiction Prose

Non-fiction Prose: Teacher's Notes

What to Teach: this focuses on three areas which require particular attention: Content, Language and Layout. It summarises the ideas, attitudes, technical terms, and so on, that will be encountered in the Student's Book. A series of OHTs is available to facilitate the teaching of Content and Language. (See page 72)

Using this Unit: this page of teacher's notes sets out how to make optimum use of this set of resources. See page 66

Role-play Activity: this should be undertaken once all the articles have been studied. Members of the class should assume different characters from the articles and discuss and debate a thought-provoking issue.

Non-fiction Prose:
Resource Worksheets, Handouts and OHTs

2a. **'Spider Diagram' OHT:** this OHT functions as an ideal starting point, graphically illustrating the kind and range of questions that students need to be aware of when tackling the non-fiction texts. See page 68

2b. **'Some Aspects of Non-fiction Writing' OHT:** this OHT introduces students to key terms and concepts. It can be used several times; on each occasion, in fact, a new text is introduced, until the terms and concepts are well and truly embedded. See page 69

2c. **'What to Look out for in Non-fiction Writing' OHT:** this OHT focuses on key devices used for persuasion. See page 70

2d. **'Travel Writing and Autobiography' OHT:** this OHT is ideally for use with these genres – but also works with others when the teacher is seeking to distinguish between objective fact and subjective opinion. See page 71

2e. **'Newspaper Non-fiction' OHT:** this OHT should be used when teaching the Media passages, to provide a framework for analysis. See page 72

2f. **'Language' OHT:** this OHT provides an ideal approach to teaching this element, setting out six specific areas that students should be aware of. See page 73

The worksheets and handouts that follow encourage the students to work on their own (or in small groups) at a variety of stimulating tasks, directed to the set passages.

2g. **'Focusing on "A Mongolian Wedding"' Worksheet** See page 74

2h. **'A Comparison with "A Mongolian Wedding"' Handout** See page 75

2i. **'Focusing on "The Other Side of the Dale"' Worksheet** See page 77

2j. **'Focusing on "The Lady in the Van"' Worksheet** See page 79

2k. **'A Comparison with "The Lady in the Van"' Handout** See page 80

2l. **'Focusing on "Don't Leave me Here to Die"' Worksheet** See page 81

2m. **'Sport For All? – Part 1' Worksheet** See page 82

2n. **'Sport For All? – Part 2' Handout** See page 83

2o. **'Parents and Children – Part 1' Handout** See page 84

2p. **'Parents and Children – Part 2' Worksheet** See page 85

2q. **'Parents and Children – Part 3' Handout** See page 86

2r. **'Parents and Children – Part 4' Worksheet** See page 87

2s. **'Which Devices have the Writers used?' Worksheet** See page 88

WHAT TO TEACH

The three areas to particularly concentrate on when teaching non-fiction prose are:

* content
* language
* layout.

Content

It is important here to stress that writers are putting across *ideas* and *attitudes*, judgement and opinion, in this unit, rather more than the *feelings* to be encountered in fiction and poetry.

Students will be looking at, and expected to distinguish between, fact and opinion; and will be noting an author's bias, use of exaggeration or other forms of distortion. It is important that they ask themselves who the passage is aimed at and why it has been written, as well as the more obvious questions of what it says and how it achieves its effects.

It is an interesting exercise to discuss with students how the first three passages differ from fiction – or what features travel writing and autobiography have in common with fiction, for example, the use of dialogue, the creation of character and a sense of story.

Pupils should be aware that autobiography is a personal account by the author, and may well be biased, exaggerated for comic effect or merely to make it interesting, or in other ways distorted, telescoped or conflated. It may, in fact, then, have some fictional elements without being particularly factitious. Travel writing, especially in its modern popular format, is extremely subjective, often being as much about the author and his or her interaction with people encountered as it is about the actual place visited.

Language

Here students will be expected to look not just at vocabulary and figures of speech but also at tone. Some work has been incorporated that will allow them to understand the use of coloured speech, imagery, cliché, connotation and denotation, irony, rhetorical question and subjective and objective judgements.

Layout

Although one of the areas to be examined is layout, there are very few distinctive features of this kind in this collection of passages in the *Edexcel Anthology for GCSE English*.

There are some small black and white photographs, and some subheadings and italicisation. The newspaper articles are in columns and have bold headlines, none of which (with the possible exception of the punning 'Mind Games') is particularly arresting.

It seems unlikely that students can be expected to make more than fairly obvious comments on layout. They should be able to comment briefly on structural devices such as:

* headings
* columns and font styles
* use of quotations that stand out
* paragraph length.

USING THIS UNIT

See pages 68 and 70

Before reading the non-fiction prose in the *Edexcel Anthology for GCSE English* show students the two OHTs: 2c. 'What to Look out for' and 2a. 'Spider Diagram' which ask the important how, why and who questions. Explain thoroughly the technical terms encountered. Due to the varied nature of the non-fiction prose, ranging from autobiography to newspaper features, students will find that there is no introductory section on how to 'tackle' non-fiction in the Student's Book. Other OHTs deal in more detail with language and the difference between objective fact and subjective opinion.

See page 88

The worksheets will be useful for establishing the students' understanding of the non-fiction prose.

The worksheet: 2s. 'Which Devices have the Writers used?' can be used for each of the texts and should be photocopied and distributed as the stories are studied.

There are individual worksheets on all the non-fiction texts. These can be completed as the stories are studied, or as revision exercises at the end of the course.

See pages 84–87

These pages provide stimulus material. These should be shown to the students to prompt discussion.

See page 67

To round off the course there is a role-play activity on all the newspaper articles using characters from all of the different articles.

ROLE-PLAY ACTIVITY ON THE NEWSPAPER ARTICLES

Once all of the newspaper articles have been studied, members of the class should assume each of the following 'characters':

Stanley Stewart
Miss Precious
Joseph Barclay
Miss Shepherd
Cathy O'Dowd
Duncan McNeil
'A Couch Potato'
Trevor Brooking
Benjamin Spock (some research needed)
Ben Tan ('Mind Games')

and discuss or debate the following issue:

'Encourage children to push themselves physically – in sport, outdoor pursuits, travel, and so on – and you'll have no problems bringing them up.'

✱ To what extent can outdoor activities provide the best form of discipline for a growing child?

✱ What about children who really don't like sport?

These same characters could also take questions from the audience (the rest of the class) on a variety of topical issues.

2a. SPIDER DIAGRAM

Here is a spider diagram showing what to look for in a piece of non-fiction prose and the how, why, and who questions that it is important to ask.

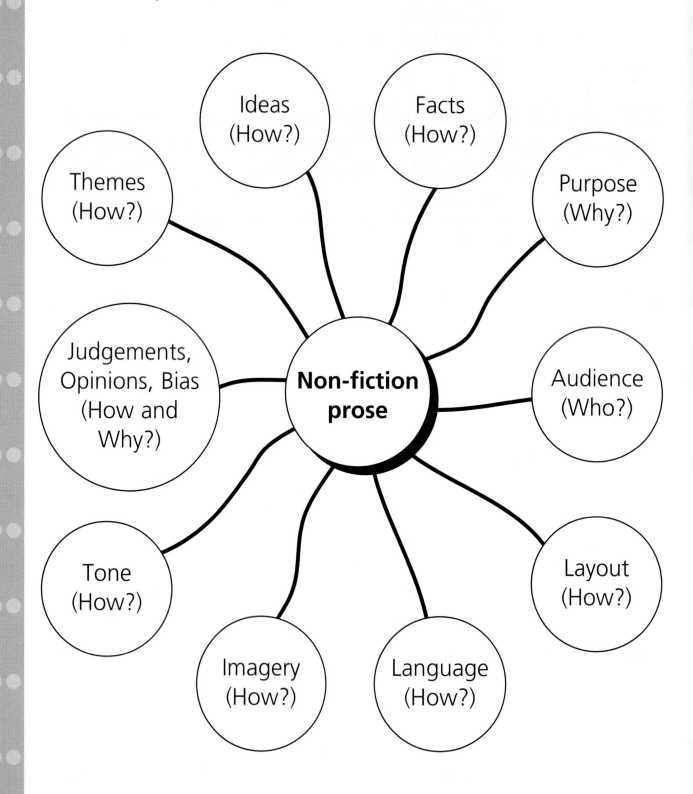

2b. SOME ASPECTS OF NON-FICTION WRITING

GENRE: the type of writing the author has chosen, for example, autobiography or travel writing.

POINT OF VIEW: the author's outlook, or overview of the subject; where he or she is 'coming from'.

REGISTER: the way a writer's use of language is influenced by what is appropriate for the purpose and context, and by the expectations and level of the audience.

TONE: the 'voice' in which the passage is intended to be read, for example, light and humorous, sad or serious.

IRONY: this is a mocking tone where the author, by saying one thing, is really suggesting its opposite.

THEMES: the general ideas that run through the passage and unify it.

THE IMPLIED: our understanding of all of the above allows us very often to see an essential point or idea which is implied rather than being spelt out for us. We sometimes call it 'reading between the lines'.

NOTE: These aspects are all interrelated, for example the choice of genre will influence the register, and the point of view will influence the tone.

2c. WHAT TO LOOK OUT FOR IN NON-FICTION WRITING

THE TITLE:

✱ Is it punchy and interesting?

✱ Is it similar to a caption or a slogan?

FACTS AND FIGURES:

✱ How are they used to support an opinion or case?

✱ Have they been used selectively?

EXPERT OPINION:

✱ Are there interviews with, or quotations from, an expert to support a case?

PERSONAL TESTIMONY OR ANECDOTE:

✱ Does the author use personal examples for support or to engage with the audience?

RHETORICAL QUESTIONS:

✱ Does the author use these type of questions to make a point?

✱ They are questions that really answer themselves rather than seek an answer.

EMOTIVE IMAGES:

✱ Does the author use 'coloured speech' to stimulate a particular emotion in the reader?

INFORMAL LANGUAGE:

✱ Does the author write in a chatty, colloquial way to engage with the reader and be interesting and persuasive?

2d. **TRAVEL WRITING AND AUTOBIOGRAPHY**

When looking at travel writing and autobiography, you should be able to tell the difference between objective and subjective elements:

OBJECTIVE FACT	SUBJECTIVE OPINION
The narrator, the characters, and their background. This includes: ✱ their status ✱ details of their appearance.	What is the author's attitude to them? What is my attitude to them?
What hard facts are you given about the context and the background?	Do I understand the narrator and the characters better by engaging with the background?
What other specific information are you given?	Do I find the information interesting, believable and necessary to my overall understanding?
What is the unusual event or aspect that the writer is giving an account of?	What is my emotional response to it?

NEWSPAPER NON-FICTION

When looking at the newspaper non-fiction, you should be able to:

✱ Tell the difference between fact and opinion.

✱ Follow the writer's argument.

✱ Identify the writer's implications, i.e. what he or she does not actually say but clearly means.

✱ Recognise bias or inconsistencies in the argument or treatment of an issue.

✱ Identify the argument's strengths or weaknesses and comment on it in other appropriate ways.

2f. LANGUAGE

When looking at the language of a passage of non-fiction (all the texts in the section), you should be able to understand and comment on:

✱ Why the writer has used the language and vocabulary in a particular way and to what purpose.

✱ How the language varies or changes.

✱ Whether it is formal, informal or mixed.

✱ How sentence lengths vary.

✱ How paragraphs are linked.

✱ What figures of speech and imagery are used.

2g. FOCUSING ON 'A MONGOLIAN WEDDING'

Having read the passage, answer these questions which will help you determine how well you understand it. You may need to use a dictionary for some of them.

Explain the expression 'unburdening themselves with pre-emptive confessions' in line 2.
Comment on the humour in paragraph 3.
What was the mood of the bride and bridegroom in each other's company? Why was this?
Why did the writer suggest to the interpreter that she should not correctly translate his song?
What does the writer think of the best man?
Explain the expression 'a proprietorial interest' in line 76?
Explain the humour in the caricature of Wyatt Earp.
How did the brawl come about?
What was the mood after the brawl ended?
Why does the author think the mixture of 'camaraderie' and 'violence' was a 'rather healthy business'?

74

2h.

FOR COMPARISON WITH 'A MONGOLIAN WEDDING'

Reginald Teague-Jones's 'Adventures in Persia' is an account of a 3,000-mile car journey from Beirut to India, in 1926. In this extract, the author and his hired help stop at a café and enter it.

For a few minutes my eyes smarted and watered and my lungs nearly choked with the fumes and smoke. Then gradually I began to discern figures seated on low stools at rough wooden benches or tables. These were the owners of the animals outside, and the steady murmur of their voices as they exchanged the gossip of the road was punctuated by the bubbling of the water in the *qalian* bowls.

Viewed in the murky half-light, the effect was almost eerie, as one muffled figure after another would reach over, grasp the stem of the *qalian*, raise the mouthpiece to his lips and inhale deeply. He would fill his lungs to coughing point with the pungent fumes and then exhale slowly and deliberately a jet of bluish-grey smoke.

Abdul and I seated ourselves on a couple of spare stools, and ordered a glass of tea each.

'*Bi-chashm!* By my eyes!' The *ghulam*, or servant of the teahouse, took my order. Through the thick haze I could discern the dull yellow light of the tarnished brass samovar, heroic in its dimensions and kept permanently on the boil to provide hot water for the tea.

I watched the *ghulam* produce a couple of small tea-glasses, and hoped they had been washed after the last user. He poured into each a little tea from a diminutive chinaware pot, and then filled them up with boiling water from the samovar. Sugar was added, and the resulting beverage was hot, sweet and refreshing. I sipped it with a sense of satisfaction, tempered by the thought that the water, before going into the samovar, had been collected in a kerosene tin from the *joob* (water channel) outside. It was mere chance that, as we came out from the stifling atmosphere of the tea-house, and I murmured something to Abdul about the refreshing effects of a glass of hot tea, my eyes fell on the *joob*. There, floating in the very middle of it, was a dead cat.

WRITING ACTIVITY

Consider:

∗ the author's use of foreign words to add realism.

∗ his eye for detail and his attempts to add atmosphere.

∗ his dry sense of humour.

∗ how this old-fashioned style of travel writing is different from Stanley Stewart's.

Which account do you feel is likely to tell you more about foreign countries and cultures?

2h. FOR COMPARISON WITH 'A MONGOLIAN WEDDING'

continued

Notice how the same author chooses to describe an interesting character he meets:

He was the biggest and most picturesque specimen of a Kurd I had ever seen outside of a picture-book. His size was enhanced by the lofty native head-dress. I expected to find him armed to the teeth, but his only visible weapon was a silver-hilted *khanjar*, or dagger, which protruded from the multifolds of his waistband.

More impressive than the dagger, however, was a large *qalian*, or water-pipe. It was a fine specimen of noble proportions, and would not have been unworthy of the Shah himself. It had an intricately carved silver top-piece to hold the tobacco and a very elaborately decorated water bowl. The mouthpiece was probably amber. It marked the owner as a person of importance, a tribal chief, perhaps.

The Kurd was squatting comfortably on his bed with the *qalian* propped up beside him, which is how I had such a clear view of it. He was inhaling great mouthfuls of smoke, drawing it deep down into his lungs, and then exhaling it in long blue streamers which curled up towards the solitary electric light bulb hanging from the ceiling. The bulb was dirty and flyblown and gave out a pallid flickering light that threatened to fail at any moment.

✱ Is the Kurd a caricature?

✱ How is this type of characterisation and scene-setting different from Stanley Stewart's?

✱ Which is the more vivid and realistic?

✱ Which style do you prefer?

✱ How does this type of characterisation differ from Stanley Stewart's?

2i. FOCUSING ON 'THE OTHER SIDE OF THE DALE'

Having read the passage, answer these questions which will help you determine how well you understand it. You may need to use a dictionary for some of them.

It is quite clear that the discussion between a Headteacher and a school inspector about a particular pupil should be confidential.

✱ Do you think this episode actually took place in this form?

✱ Isn't it likely that Gervase Phinn actually changed names and settings?

✱ What other steps might he have taken to prevent places and individuals being identified?

What does this tell us about this genre? How much of this do you imagine is actually non-fiction in the strictest sense?

What is the writer's opinion of the view from the classroom window? Consider especially lines 13–14, 'It was a grim and gloomy picture but, at the same time, quite awesome.'

What is surprising about the way Joseph Richard Barclay speaks to the author? Consider the author's response, 'You're quite the expert, aren't you, Joseph?' on line 44.

2i. FOCUSING ON 'THE OTHER SIDE OF THE DALE'

continued

What does the word 'precocious' from line 53 mean? Look it up in a dictionary if necessary. From the evidence in the passage, do you agree with this judgement of the pupil?

Find the simile that characterises Miss Precious's relationship with her pupil. Explain what you understand by it and why it seems appropriate.

Why is the author amused to see Mrs Durden going on duty in the playground? What provisions does she make for the occasion?

How would you describe Captain Mac? Briefly (in two or three lines) summarise his character.

What does the word 'eccentric' mean in line 154? What do you understand by the expression 'dyed-in-the-wool'?

What does it mean to be 'hale and hearty' (line 178)? What does the 'old-fashioned turn of phrase' tell us about the speaker?

Comment on the effectiveness of the simile that characterises Joseph in line 210.

2j. FOCUSING ON 'THE LADY IN THE VAN'

Having read the extract from *Writing Home*, answer these questions which will help you determine how well you understand it. You may need to use a dictionary for some of them.

Explain what the author means by 'Happy to run to a new (albeit old) van' in line 2.
Why do you imagine, when the author didn't mention the van to visitors, they didn't refer to it either (lines 21–22)?
Why is it amusing that Miss Shepherd should tell Vincent Price to 'Pipe down' (line 31)?
Explain the dramatic manner with which Miss Shepherd would emerge from her van.
Explain the expression 'her querulous and often resentful demeanour' in line 65.
What does the conversation with the social worker tell us about Miss Shepherd's character?
Do you think Miss Shepherd could have become a nun? Consider the qualities required and whether or not Miss Shepherd had any of them.
What impression do we form of the author from this extract?
Find an incident from the passage which you suspect the author might have exaggerated.
Comment on any expression which you found interesting and effective. Give your reasons.

2k. A COMPARISON WITH 'THE LADY IN THE VAN'

Below is an extract from Alan Bennett's play, *The Lady in the Van*. Read it and then answer the questions which follow.

A. Bennett	I thought you were in the van.
Miss Shepherd	No, I was in the terrace, on the pavement. The air's better there.
A. Bennett	Somebody's been banging on the side of the van.
Miss Shepherd	Oh yes? What did he want?
A. Bennett	I don't know what he wanted. Thumping, probably.
Miss Shepherd	He wasn't a Catholic gentleman of refined appearance?
A. Bennett	No. He was a lout.
Miss Shepherd	He may have been wanting a pencil. Or a pamphlet possibly. When you provide a service you do get these callers.
A. Bennett	Miss Shepherd. This was a hooligan.
Miss Shepherd	Some people might say I was a tramp. It's just want of perception. You rub people up the wrong way. You should be like me, take people as they come.

Alan Bennett goes as a woman appears carrying a bag of clothes.

Social Worker	Miss Shepherd. I'm Jane, the social worker.
Miss Shepherd	I don't want the social worker. I'm about to listen to *Any Answers*.
Social Worker	I've brought you some clothes. You wrote asking for a coat.
Miss Shepherd	Not during *Any Answers*. I'm a busy woman. I only asked for one coat.
Social Worker	I brought three, in the event you fancied a change.
Miss Shepherd	Where am I supposed to put three coats? Besides, I was planning on washing this coat in the not too distant future, so that makes four. My wardrobe's driving me mad.
Social Worker	This is my old nursing mac.
Miss Shepherd	I have a mac. Besides, green isn't my colour. Have you got a stick?
Social Worker	The council have that in hand. It's been precepted for.
Miss Shepherd	Will it be long enough?
Social Worker	Yes. It's one of our special sticks.
Miss Shepherd	I don't want a special stick. I want an ordinary stick. Only longer. Does it have one of those rubber things on it?
Social Worker	I imagine so.
Miss Shepherd	It has to have a rubber thing. It's no earthly use to me without the rubber thing, as you'd know if you weren't so young. I hope you're bona fide. You have a look of someone foreign.
Social Worker	I'm just new. Is it all right if I call from time to time?
Miss Shepherd	Not during *Any Answers*. And *Petticoat Line* is another programme I tune in for. They'll sometimes have discussion on the Common Market from a woman's point of view.
Social Worker	If I should want to get in touch with you whom should I call?
Miss Shepherd	I don't want to be got in touch with.
Social Worker	There must be someone.
Miss Shepherd	You can try Mr Bennett, only don't take any notice of what he says. He's a communist, possibly.
A. Bennett	Me? Did you ask the people opposite? They're nearer.
Social Worker	They said they didn't relate to her. You were the one she related to.
A. Bennett	Is that what they said ... 'related to'?
Social Worker	No. That's me. They said you were her pal. She was your girlfriend. They didn't mean that, obviously.
A. Bennett	No.

WRITING ACTIVITY

* What does this extract add to our understanding of Miss Shepherd?
* How does her discussion with the social worker compare with Bennett's account of it in the anthologised piece?
* What do we learn of Alan Bennett?

21. FOCUSING ON 'DON'T LEAVE ME HERE TO DIE'

Having read the passage, answer these questions which will help you determine how well you understand it. You may need to use a dictionary for some of them.

Explain why rescuing someone on Everest was not straightforward.
What does the word 'incapacitated' mean?
What went through the author's mind when she found the injured climber?
Why did she feel as if she was 'glimpsing a possible future for myself'?
Why was she 'both encouraged and appalled'?
Explain why the injured climber had removed some clothing.
In what respects were Fran and Serguei ill-equipped for the climb?
Comment on the effectiveness of the simile 'as useless as strands of spaghetti'.
Why did the writer find that the thought of going on had become 'intolerable'?
What was the effect on the author of the injured climber being female?

2m. SPORT FOR ALL? – PART 1

1 Note down the positive and negative effects of sport in schools, mentally, physically and financially, as demonstrated in the four newspaper articles.

Make a note of which article you take the information from and include quotations where appropriate. You should also consider which effects are long term and which are short term. Use the table below as a guide.

	POSITIVE EFFECTS	NEGATIVE EFFECTS
Mentally	For example, sport stimulates the brain so that . . .	For example, bullying . . . For example, humiliation . . .
Physically	For example, exercise is essential for health because . . .	For example, bullying . . .
Financially	For example, sports can make vast sums of money . . .	For example, sport can cost a lot of money . . . For example, some 'student-athletes' are not making the grade . . .

2 Look at the list of words and expressions below. Which of them is appropriate to each article's viewpoint and tone?

in favour of school sport	impressionistic
subjective	biased
makes personal confession	flippant
serious-minded	objective
uses exaggeration	hard-hitting
light-hearted	against school sport
makes use of anecdotal or personal experience	highly researched

Look up any words you don't completely understand. Find at least three words or expressions for each article.

3 What are the attitudes to sport of the four writers (John Harris, Julian Borger, Wendy Berliner and Duncan McNeil)?

2n. SPORT FOR ALL? – PART 2

WRITING ACTIVITY

1 School sport is an issue much debated at the moment. Do you agree that it is such an important issue as to warrant press and television attention?

2 Having read the four passages, which do you feel you agree with and disagree with most strongly? In both cases, explain your answer.

3 Consider the title of the article by John Harris.

The word 'horrors' has a double meaning. It is used humorously to express a child's 'trauma' at the thought of 'forward rolls', but also refers to a more serious matter.

Read the two passages by John Harris and Julian Borger again and make a note of any 'real' horrors resulting from school sport.

4 Julian Borger believes that US colleges are 'addicted' to the wealth that sport teams make for them. Consider this aspect of sport. Do you agree with the amount of money that soccer (or football) generates? You may wish to think about the English FA Premiership.

5 What do you think Julian Borger means by 'there is a price to be paid for taking student sports too seriously'?

6 What is the 'transatlantic difference' referred to by Julian Borger?

Consider the attitudes to sport, suggested in the articles, of: Germans, English, Americans and Scots.

What does this tell us about the significance of the issue of sport in schools?

7 The articles by John Harris and Duncan McNeil MSP are written from the point of view of adults looking back at their own experiences of sport in school.

Why does Duncan McNeil believe sport in school wasn't as important when he was a boy? Think about his comment 'But how times have changed'.

What effect has the modern change in lifestyle had? Do you agree with Duncan McNeil about this?

Why does John Harris think school sport is 'nonsense'?

8 Imagine your school field was being (or had been) sold. Write a letter to your local MP to complain. You should give reasons why you object.

2o. PARENTS AND CHILDREN – PART 1

Stimulus Material

An effective and stimulating way into the 'Parents and Children' section is to discuss the following apparent contradictions:

What teenagers can and cannot do is very confusing.

* At 12, you are not allowed to have a job – but you have to pay full fare on an aeroplane.

* At 13, you can get a part-time job but you're not old enough to go into a pub.

* At 14, you can now go in a pub with an adult but not to drink alcohol – even though you can drink at home.

* At 15, you can be sentenced to youth custody but cannot have sex (legally) and you still can't go in a pub by yourself – or buy a national lottery ticket.

* At 16, you can now have legal sex but you cannot consent to marriage. You can join the Armed Forces but you still can't drink in a pub (or buy alcohol anywhere), even though you are allowed to smoke in one.

* At 17, you can hold a driving licence but not hire a car. You can be put on probation but you're not allowed to vote. You may be working but many banks will not give you a credit card.

* At 18, you can have a drink in a pub and you can serve on a jury. You can go into a sex shop and a betting shop. You can buy a house, but not stand as an MP or a Local Councillor, even though you can now vote for one.

SPEAKING & LISTENING

Discuss these inconsistencies and confusions.

* What would you like to see changed?

* Is there any reason for things being the way they are?

* Are any of these inconsistencies inevitable and likely to remain?

* Can you think of any other examples like the above?

2p. PARENTS AND CHILDREN – PART 2

'Parents Learn how to Say NO'

* Put 'the permissive gospels of postwar childcare gurus' in simple English.

* What do you understand by 'the *laisser-faire* approach to childrearing'?

* How does Steve Biddulph think adults should bring up children?

* What do you understand by the term 'Time-out'?

* What appears to be the author's opinion on the way parents should discipline their children?

'Pay your Children too much Attention . . .'

* What do you understand by the term 'hot-housing'?

* What is Zero to Three's belief about the effects of overstimulation of children?

* What are 'verbal and cognitive skills'?

* What is the difference between 'quality time' and 'unhurried time' in the context of this article?

* In what respect can overstimulation be 'a form of child abuse'?

'Use Persuasion not Coercion'

* Do you think the author is right that the only person who smacks children is 'a parent with a lousy temper out of control'?

* Explain the expression 'cajole and manipulate' as the author is using it.

* Comment on the effectiveness of the metaphor, 'has bulldozed through that line'.

* What is the author's view of 'criminalizing even the smack on the leg'?

* What does she mean when she says 'the law is simply unenforceable'?

'Smacking not the answer', Say Kids

* Explain the point that Paul McAteer is making.

* Why does Hugo McIlveen think that smacking children 'is sort of barbaric'?

* Is Sheena Hall exaggerating when she says some parents 'use their children as punchbags'?

* How does the NSPCC view the issue of smacking?

* Summarise Chris King's position. Do you agree with it?

2q. **PARENTS AND CHILDREN – PART 3**

 WRITING ACTIVITY

Use the quotations in the boxes below to help you to write a speech on the view that 'Persuasion not coercion is the best form of discipline for children.'

'The word "discipline", which had virtually disappeared from child care manuals of the past two decades, is reappearing in family magazines and a stream of bestselling "how to" parenting manuals.'

'TWENTY YEARS AGO SWEDEN BANNED THE SMACKING OF CHILDREN. THERE HAS BEEN OVERWHELMING SUPPORT FOR THE MOVE AND A MARKED REDUCTION IN SERIOUS CHILD ABUSE CASES.'

'It's my kid. I know what's best for him. I'll smack him when he needs smacking!'

'Parents don't want all that controlling stuff that comes with old-fashioned discipline. What they want is to be able to discipline their children through teaching them and encouraging them.'

'To pass a law against smacking toddlers is a ludicrious intervention into one of the most intimate and private relationships.'

2r. PARENTS AND CHILDREN – PART 4

1 Look at the list of words and expressions below. Which of them is appropriate to each article's viewpoint and tone?

in favour of disciplining children	impressionistic
subjective	biased
makes personal confession	flippant
serious-minded	objective
uses exaggeration	hard-hitting
light-hearted	against disciplining children
humorous	highly researched
makes use of anecdotal or personal experience	

Look up any words you don't completely understand. Find at least three words or expressions for each article.

2 What are the attitudes of the three writers and the reporters from the *Children's Express* to bringing up children?

ALEXANDRA FREAN'S ATTITUDE:
CHERRY NORTON'S ATTITUDE:
MADELEINE BUNTING'S ATTITUDE:
THE *CHILDREN'S EXPRESS* REPORTERS' ATTITUDES:

2s. WHICH DEVICES HAVE THE WRITERS USED?

TITLE	EXAMPLE	EFFECT
Humour		
Irony		
Repetition		
Rhetorical question		
Exaggeration		
Coloured speech		
Persuasive words or phrases		

3 Different Cultures and Traditions

Different Cultures and Traditions: Teacher's Notes

What to Teach: this focuses on areas which require particular attention, and gives advice on how best to explore the short stories with the use of the material provided. A series of OHTs is available to facilitate the teaching of form and content. *See page 91*

Using this Unit: this page of teacher's notes sets out how to make optimum use of this set of resources. *See page 92*

Different Cultures and Traditions: Resource Worksheets, Handouts and OHTs

3a. **'Reading in Four Stages' OHT:** this OHT suggests a stepped approach to reading, which leads to in-depth knowledge. *See page 93*

3b. **'What to Look out for in Short Stories' OHT:** this OHT introduces the students to the key terms and concepts which will be explored with use of the OHTs in this unit. This OHT and the others may be used several times; on each occasion, in fact, a new text is introduced until the terms and concepts are well and truly embedded. *See page 93*

3c. **'Types of Narrative OHT:** this OHT encourages students to distinguish between first- and third- person narrators, and their differing viewpoints. *See page 94*

3d. **'Characters' OHT:** this OHT provides an ideal framework for character analysis, and a blueprint for a character-study essay. *See page 95*

3e. **'Place' OHT** and **3f. 'Time' OHT:** these two OHTs emphasise the importance of a story's setting and background, particularly with regard to the cultural context. *See page 96*

3g. **'Language and Structure' OHT:** this OHT provides a focus for an area of the examination which often appears difficult to students, but which need not be. It also suggests a format for a Language Log that students should be encouraged to complete for every story. *See page 97*

3h. **'About the Authors' Handout:** this is an information sheet giving biographical information which students should find interesting, bearing in mind the need to 'read' the stories in their cultural context. *See pages 98 and 99*

The worksheets that follow are provided for all the stories, to stimulate interest, to aid textual exploration and to accumulate revision material.

3i. **'Character Comparison Log' Worksheet** *See page 100*

3j. **'Understanding the Stories' Worksheet** *See page 101*

3k. **'Comparisons: 'Country Lovers' vs. 'Veronica' Worksheet** *See page 102*

3l. **'Comparisons: 'The Schoolteacher's Guest' vs. 'Vendetta' – Part 1 Worksheet** *See page 103*

3m. **'Comparisons: 'The Schoolteacher's Guest' vs. 'Vendetta' – Part 2 Worksheet** *See page 104*

3n. **'Comparisons: 'The Schoolteacher's Guest' vs. 'Vendetta' – Part 3 Worksheet** *See page 105*

3o. **'Complication Chart' Worksheet** *See page 106*

3p. **'Country Lovers' Worksheet** *See page 107*

3q. **'Questions about the Stories' Handout:** this resource encourages the students to work on their own (or in groups) on a variety of stimulating tasks. See page 108

WHAT TO TEACH

When teaching short stories try to focus on the form as well as the content of the short story. Make the teaching active and take students through the structures and conventions of the short story, in particular the use of symbols and surprising denouements.

Since the examination questions will require them to look at two complete stories, spend time working on comparisons. Comparisons are not specifically required, but the best students will make them anyway.

✱ Spend time looking at the openings of two comparable stories (for example, 'Vendetta' and 'The Schoolteacher's Guest').

✱ Get students to rewrite these openings in different styles, using a different narrative technique and adapting different tenses. Work with them actively on the first sentence or two.

✱ Explore, using the OHT provided, how authors create and build up characters and setting.

✱ Let them explore the themes, drawing their own conclusions and making their own inferences. Point out that this is how it should be and there is no single, prescriptive reading.

✱ Look at the ways tension is introduced and maintained – often with a single, discordant word or phrase.

✱ Explore the stories' structure by dividing them into sections and shuffling these sections around.

✱ Examine the links between one section and another.

✱ Change the sentence order in a single paragraph and have them rewrite it as they feel is natural and most informative.

✱ Encourage personal response by brainstorming and role-play activities.

✱ Remember that students work best in pairs or groups when tackling small, controlled, specific activities, based on a relatively short passage of stimulus.

Six OHTs have been provided to assist the teaching of what constitutes a short story and the techniques the writer has employed. The first, '3a. Reading in Four Stages', is intended to help pupils to master the art of effective reading.

Students will enjoy working on the stories, and discussing their themes and implications, in groups. A number of self-explanatory logs and charts have been included to help them with their work, to act as revision material later on and as a means of recording something in concrete form of the many group discussions. The questions provided tend to be simpler than those in the Student's Book and can be used as revision material or during the actual teaching to supplement and complement.

USING THIS UNIT

See page 93

Before reading the short stories in the *Edexcel Anthology for GCSE English*, show students the two OHTs: 3a. 'Reading in Four Stages' and 3b. 'What to Look out for in Short Stories'. Also read through with them pages 118–119 in the Student's Book, 'Tackling a Short Story', so that they are aware of what to look out for when they begin studying the individual stories. Explain thoroughly the technical terms encountered. Other OHTs deal in more detail with the individual components of the stories – narrative, character, place and time, and language and structure.

See pages 101 and 106

The worksheets will be useful for establishing the students' understanding of the short stories. 3j. 'Understanding the Stories' requires students to answer the important questions brought to their attention in the Student's Book: 'Tackling a Short Story'. This should be photocopied, along with 3o. 'Complication Chart', and distributed as the stories are studied.

The other worksheets involve the comparison of two stories and should be completed after both the stories named have been studied.

See pages 98–99

3h. 'About the Authors' gives background information on the authors of the short stories included in the *Edexcel Anthology for GCSE English*. These details will be useful for establishing the context of the stories.

See page 108

At the end of the unit you will find two pages of questions on the stories (3q. 'Questions about the Stories'). These are revision exercises to be completed at the end of the course, although, alternatively, they can be used whilst studying to further aid the students as they work through the stories.

3a. READING IN FOUR STAGES

Before you can meaningfully discuss a story or write about it, you need to go through these four stages:

Stage One: Preview

* Read it in 5 minutes or less.
* Get an outline of the main story and the characters.

Stage Two: Look at The Beginning and the End

* These are the most important parts of the story.
* Compare the opening situation with where things stand at the end.

Stage Three: Skim-read

* Skim-read through the story again.
* Try to identify the **complication** – the springboard of the story where something goes wrong.

Stage Four: In-depth Study

* Re-read slowly.
* Take it all in.
* Notice the themes and conflicts.
* See what happens to the characters.
* What do they learn about **themselves/life/society**?
* What do you emotionally react to?
* Does it put across a moral or message?

3b. WHAT TO LOOK OUT FOR IN SHORT STORIES

* Narrative Voice
* Story and Plot
* Characters
* Time and Place
* Theme
* Structure and Language

3c. TYPES OF NARRATIVE

First Person

✳ The storyteller, or narrator, speaks about himself as 'I' and describes others externally.

✳ The narrator is usually a participating character in the story, very often the most important one.

✳ We find out the narrator's thoughts and feelings, but not those of the other characters.

✳ The narrator often seems to be as ignorant about what is coming next as the reader is.

Third Person

✳ The storyteller, or narrator, is a 'voice' rather than a person.

✳ The narrator refers to the characters as 'he', 'she' or 'they', and seems to have an overview of the events but no involvement in them.

✳ The narrator seems to know the thoughts, feelings and motives of the characters.

✳ The narrator knows all the outcomes from the very beginning – but teases the reader by holding things back.

3d. CHARACTERS

We judge a person's character by a combination of the following:

| **Writer Stating** | ✱ What they look like. |
| | ✱ What the narrator tells us. |

Writer Showing	✱ What they say.
	✱ What they do.
	✱ Any differences between what they say and what they do.

Reader's Interpretation	✱ What others say/think about them.
	✱ Whether or not they are consistent in their actions.
	✱ Any changes that take place in them.
	✱ The extent to which we identify with them.

Get a clear picture in your mind of the major characters.

> Think about:
>
> ✱ their appearance and personality
> ✱ their motives
> ✱ their beliefs and interests
> ✱ their relationships.

Always ask yourself:

✱ Are they fully rounded?

✱ Are they one-dimensional or shadowy?

✱ Do you feel you know enough about them to form judgements?

✱ Could you predict how they would handle a particular situation?

✱ What would they do in a crisis?

95

3e. PLACE

* The settings/backgrounds/locations are vital to our understanding of the stories. They provide us with a context for the action.

* The settings also affect the characters and their actions.

* The stories would not 'work' in the same ways if the surroundings were changed. Can you imagine them taking place in England? Or in big cities rather than rural communities? In 'Veronica', for example, the deaths of Veronica, her husband and her baby are caused by 'the squalor of village life'.

* We usually gain a strong mental picture of the location from the descriptions the authors give.

* Sometimes the stories move from one place to another, as in 'The Gold Cadillac'. You should think about the description of both places – are they described in equal detail?

3f. TIME

* The stories take place within a particular period in history – for example, the Apartheid in Africa, or the culture of racism in the American Deep South in the 1950s.

* The stories would lose a lot of their point or impact if transferred to another time. You should think about what the effect would be of setting them in modern times.

* Some of the stories are told in a straight timeline from beginning to end. Others, for example 'The Schoolteacher's Revenge', use flashbacks.

* Many of the stories span across a large number of years – 'Country Lovers' starts with Paulus and Njabulo as small children and ends with them aged 19 and 20. The writers compress events, passing over months or years almost in a single sentence.

3g. LANGUAGE AND STRUCTURE

When you look at the author's use of language you should always ask:

✳ Is it simple and straightforward?

✳ Does it have any words or mannerisms that belong to its cultural background (e.g. the Afrikaans' words in 'Country Lovers')? This adds to the realistic atmosphere of the story.

✳ Does it use slang or colloquial language? Think about differences between the way 'lois speaks to her family and the way she narrates the story in 'The Gold Cadillac'.

✳ Is it complicated and mature? Look, for example, at the opening paragraphs of 'Vendetta'.

✳ Is the language varied? Writers use short sentences and short paragraphs to build up **tension** and **suspense**. Long sentences and paragraphs have a calming effect.

It may help you to construct a language log for your stories, similar to the one below:

Title of Story: 'Vendetta'

DESCRIPTION	VIVID LANGUAGE
Metaphor suggesting the fortified nature of the setting.	'A small, mean house on the ramparts of Bonifacio' (lines 1–2)
Simile capturing image of houses high and slightly menacing.	'They looked like the nests of birds of prey' (line 9)

3h.   ABOUT THE AUTHORS

Here is some background information on the authors of the short stories. How do you think the context of each writer's life and work adds to an understanding of their story?

Nadine Gordimer

Nadine Gordimer was born in 1923, in Springs, a small mining town about 30 miles from Johannesburg. Although of Jewish origins, her earliest education was at a local convent school run by Dominican nuns. From the ages of 11 to 16, however, she was tutored at home because of a minor heart complaint. She later spent a year at university.

Gordimer's earliest short stories and novels are about the daily grind of the poor white class she herself belonged to. Her mature work dealt increasingly with the plight of the black underclass and of the unfairness of the apartheid and censorship. Several of her books were banned in her native country.

In 1991, she shared the money she received for the Nobel Prize with the Congress of South African Writers and the African National Congress, to promote libraries and scholarships.

Adewale Maja-Pearce

Adewale Maja-Pearce was born in 1953 in London, but grew up in Lagos in Nigeria, returning to England only to supplement his education and read African Studies for a Master of Arts degree at the School of Oriental and African Studies. Not a great deal is commonly known about this African writer and journalist but he has held various notable positions in the literary world, and is presently Series Editor of the African Writers Series and Africa Editor of the journal *Index on Censorship*. He observed and wrote during the Rwandan refugee crises.

Isabel Allende

Isabel Allende was born in 1942 in Lima, Peru, but was raised in Bolivia, Europe and the Middle East, moving to Chile at age 3. She worked as a journalist in Chile for several years but, after the 1973 military coup, in which her uncle, Chilean President Salvador Allende, was assassinated, she fled with her husband, son and daughter to Venezuela.

She is now one of Latin America's leading female writers, and through wide translation, her work has won international critical acclaim. Her first novel to come to popular attention, *The House of Spirits*, recounted the struggles of a Chilean family in the midst of Chile's brutal past. Through her writing she actively promotes Feminist issues and deals with Feminism in a political, historical and social context.

Mildred Taylor

Mildred Taylor was born in 1943, in Jackson, one of the largest towns in Mississippi. However, during and after World War II her family gradually migrated to the industrial north, settling in Toledo, Ohio, where she was educated.

3h. ABOUT THE AUTHORS

continued

After graduating from the University of Toledo, she spent two years in Ethiopia with the Peace Corps teaching English and History. While living in Africa, she was moved by the natural dignity and self-respect of the locals, which reminded her of stories told by her father of the slavery and deprivation that had failed to break her race's spirit. On her return to the United States, in addition to recruiting and teaching for the Peace Corps, Taylor studied journalism at the University of Colorado, where she received an MA.

During this time she was influential with the Black Student Alliance and facilitated the creation of a Black Studies course at the university. Eventually, she moved to Los Angeles where she worked during the day and wrote during the evenings and nights. Her numerous awards for writing include the Newberry Medal and Outstanding Book of the Year from the *New York Times*, and she is most famous for her celebrated books concerning the Logan family, including *Song of the Trees*, *Roll of Thunder, Hear My Cry*, and *Let the Circle be Unbroken*.

Amrita Pritam

Amrita Pritam was born in 1919 in Gujranwala, in the Punjab, a part of India which later became Pakistan. In 1947, when India was partitioned, she moved to New Delhi and began to write in Hindi – before later switching to her native Punjabi. ('The Stench of Kerosene' is translated from the original Punjabi.)

She is the author of several novels – including *Skeleton*, a deeply moving account of the Partition of India – and numerous books of short stories and poetry. Since 1960 her work has become much more Feminist in outlook, drawing on her own unhappy experiences of marriage and divorce.

Guy de Maupassant

Henri-René-Albert-Guy de Maupassant was born in 1850 at the Chateau de Miromesnil, near Dieppe in Normandy. Even though this 'stately home' was not the property of his parents, being merely rented to mark the happy occasion, the family's aristocratic traditions cannot be doubted, nobility having been granted to them by the Habsburg Empire in the previous century.

Having been educated by his mother during his early life, Guy attended a Catholic boarding school from the age of 13, where he was desperately unhappy, and from which he was eventually expelled for penning a licentious poem. However, he was academically successful and went to Paris in 1869 to read for a degree in law, unfortunately interrupted by his voluntary service in the French Army.

Between 1872 and 1880, he worked as a civil servant, and the mass of his literary material was produced in the period between 1880 and 1890. The author, who claimed all of his stories were based on his own real-life experiences, is celebrated as France's greatest writer of short stories. He visited Corsica in 1880 and 'Vendetta' was one of several stories inspired by the trip.

3i. CHARACTER COMPARISON LOG

LINE REF.	STORY TITLE:	STORY TITLE:
	Name:	Name:
	Physical characteristics:	Physical characteristics:
	Personality:	Personality:
	Important events in their life:	Important events in their life:
	Importance in story:	Importance in story:

3j. UNDERSTANDING THE STORIES

Having read the stories, begin to fill in this chart which will help you to recognise and understand the key components of the stories. You can return to this chart and add more as your knowledge of the stories grows.

Title of story ....

What do you think is the significance of the title?	
How does the beginning grab your attention and make you want to keep reading?	
Who is narrating the story? What type of narrative is it? Why do you think the author has chosen this type?	
What is the complication?	
How do you imagine the setting, based on the evidence of the story? What effect do the setting, time, period and culture have on the characters?	
Do you think there is a lesson to be learnt from the story? If so, what?	
What type of language does the author use (for example, emotive, matter-of-fact, poetic)? Do you think it is effective?	
What is the climax of the story? Do you think there is an anti-climax? If so, what is it?	
How does the story end? Do you like the ending? How would you have ended it?	
Do you like the story? Why (or why not)?	

3k. COMPARISONS: 'COUNTRY LOVERS' vs. 'VERONICA'

'COUNTRY LOVERS'	'VERONICA'
Background and setting	
The main characters: their background and personality	
Relationships: how main characters feel at beginning	
How do their relationships change?	
What role do education, race and gender play?	

31. COMPARISONS: 'THE SCHOOLTEACHER'S GUEST' vs. 'VENDETTA' – PART 1

'THE SCHOOLTEACHER'S GUEST'	'VENDETTA'
Ines's attitude to her son's death:	The widow Saverini's attitude to her son's death:
The community's attitude towards the death:	The communtity's attitude towards the death:
Agua Santa – description and culture:	Bonifacio – description and culture:
Ines's attitude to revenge:	Widow Saverini's attitude to revenge:
The mango farmer: what do we know of him?	Nicolas Ravolati: what do we know of him?
The methods used by Ines to avoid being caught:	The methods used by the widow Saverini to avoid being caught:

3m. COMPARISONS: 'THE SCHOOLTEACHER'S GUEST' vs. 'VENDETTA' – PART 2

Ines has a firm belief that fate will help her to bring about revenge. The widow Saverini works with determination to bring it about herself. Compare the attitudes and personalities of the two characters. Write your answers below.

INES	THE WIDOW SAVERINI

Make a list of the similarities between the two stories in the boxes below.

'THE SCHOOLTEACHER'S GUEST'	'VENDETTA'
Plot	Plot
Setting	Setting
Theme	Theme

3n. COMPARISONS: 'THE SCHOOLTEACHER'S GUEST' vs. 'VENDETTA' – PART 3

In 'The Schoolteacher's Guest' it seems everyone in the village knew about the act of revenge. In 'Vendetta', no one knew. What does this tell us about the differing communities? Give reasons for your answers below.

Is revenge justified when the law proves inadequate?

Briefly discuss this with reference to both short stories. Write your answer below.

3o. COMPLICATION CHART

Here is a chart for you to record the 'complication' of all six stories and the characters involved. Remember the complication is the element where something 'goes wrong' and triggers off the main action.

SHORT STORY	COMPLICATION	CHARACTERS INVOLVED

3p.   COUNTRY LOVERS

Cut out and re-arrange these seven sentences from 'Country Lovers', trying to put them in their best and logical order. When you have finished, compare your effort with the original on page 70 of the *Edexcel Anthology for GCSE English* and discuss what you think this brief episode adds to the story.

Thebedi did not ask him in.

The women were away on the lands, weeding, as they were employed to do as casual labour in summer; only the very old remained, propped up on the ground outside the huts in the flies and the sun.

The child had not been well; it had diarrhoea.

Two days later, when his mother and father had left the farm for the day, he appeared again.

He went into Njabulo's house, where the child lay; she did not follow but stayed outside the door and watched without seeing an old crone who had lost her mind, talking to herself, talking to the fowls who ignored her.

She said, 'The milk comes from me.'

He asked her where its food was.

3q. QUESTIONS ABOUT THE STORIES

Here are some questions about the short stories that you could discuss in groups or write about.

'Country Lovers'

1 At some point, the relationship between Paulus and Thebedi becomes a physical one. (Sexual relations between black and white people were illegal in South Africa at the time under the Immorality Act.) Why does she 'not ask questions any longer' (line 72)? He now dictates when they meet. What do we learn about their changing attitudes to each other?

2 Discuss the author's use of symbolism when describing the baby's appearance. Comment on the baby's hair 'like that which carries the seeds of certain weeds in the veld' (lines 116–117).

3 What does Paulus's 'grimace of tears, anger and self-pity' (line 153) suggest? What is his attitude to 'it'? Why does he want her to 'take it away somewhere'? Is he ashamed of the baby, or ashamed of it being known that he had a relationship with a black girl?

4 We are told Thebedi 'stayed outside the door and watched' (lines 171–172) whilst Paulus went to look at his baby on the second occasion. Is there any suggestion she knew what he was doing – and was party to it? Later in court she claimed to have seen him 'pouring liquid into the baby's mouth' (line 192) and that he had threatened to shoot her. What is the explanation for all this? Is she a reliable witness?

5 What attitude is revealed by Paulus's father's reaction after the trial?

6 Consider Thebedi's summing up, 'It was a thing of our childhood' (lines 214–215). Is that an accurate description of it?

7 What is the significance of the story's title?

'Veronica'

1 Discuss how the author grabs the reader's attention in the opening 20 lines.

2 When Veronica rejects the move to the city, Okeke says 'I snapped a twig and threw it into the water. It bobbed on the current and then vanished from sight' (lines 39–40). Does this have any symbolic meaning or is it just straightforward description? What might it suggest to the reader? Now read the very last sentence of the story and compare the two images.

3 It seems significant that when Okeke does return to his home village, after being away for ten years, it is 'quite by chance' (line 59) through his work, rather than

QUESTIONS ABOUT THE STORIES

continued

through choice. He is shocked by the dirt, disease and poverty. What does all this tell us about his attitudes to his roots?

4 Consider these two statements that Okeke makes to Veronica: 'You would be better off in the city' (line 97) and 'All the women I meet are only interested in money and cars' (line 102). What do these statements tell us about the speaker? Is there a kind of contradiction in the two?

5 Consider the end of the story. Was Veronica's death inevitable? Why does she accept it as inevitable?

6 What do you think Okeke's feelings are for Veronica? Is there any suggestion of love? Base you answer on the whole story.

'The Schoolteacher's Guest'

1 Look at what the locals do to the house of the man who did the shooting (lines 37–43). Why do they take this action? What do they hope to achieve?

2 Do you think Ines has some sympathy for the 'poor', 'old man' she describes as having had 'very bad luck' (lines 98–102)? What kind of tone is she using?

3 'I had to do it. It was fate' (line 101). Ines seems to be suggesting it was the old man's destiny to be held up in Agua Santa by a shattered windscreen. She also reveals, 'I've been waiting all these years; I knew he would come sooner or later' (line 105). What do these attitudes tell us about **a)** Ines, and **b)** local attitudes to revenge?

4 Notice how the 'murderer's' old house has been overrun with an 'impenetrable jungle' (line 159). The locals hack their way into it and bury the body at the scene of the original 'crime'. Why do they choose to do this? How does it fit into their idea of justice?

5 Why might the author have subtitled her story 'a legend of justice' (line 183)? Was justice done?

'The Gold Cadillac'

1 From the first 30 lines what impression do we gain of the Black community?

2 Consider why 'lois's father was so determined to drive his new Cadillac to Mississippi, when everyone else thought it 'a mighty dangerous thing to do' (lines 155–180)?

3 What reasons did other people give against the trip?

4 Why did the police officer automatically assume that the car was stolen (line 230)?

3q. QUESTIONS ABOUT THE STORIES

continued

5 How and why did the mother and father both change their minds about the Cadillac at the end of the story?

'A Stench of Kerosene'

1 What does the expression 'they had bartered their hearts to each other' suggest about the feelings of Manak and Guleri for each other? There are three other references to the heart (lines 8, 92, 101). Discuss the use the author makes of the feelings of the heart.

2 Consider the reasons why Bhavari behaves evasively in line 75. Why does he not want to bring up the subject of the fair?

3 Guleri gives Manak his flute when he accompanies her at the start of her journey, even though he is not going to the fair. Manak particularly notices Bhavani's flute sticking out of his bundle on the way to the fair. What do the flute and the fair symbolise in the story?

4 '"Why do you croak like an old woman?" said his mother seriously. "Be a man". Manak wanted to retort, "You are a woman; why don't you cry like one for a change!" But he remained silent.' (lines 84–86). What do we learn of the relationship between Manak and his mother and their feelings towards each other from this?

5 Notice the dramatic effect of the sudden hysterical shrieking at the end. How does this contrast with Manak's mood since learning of Guleri's death?

'Vendetta'

1 What impression do you form of the widow in the first 40 lines? How do we know she is a very determined woman?

2 'The next day Antoine Saverini was buried, and soon his name ceased to be mentioned in Bonifacio' (lines 40–41). What does this tell us about local attitudes? Why is it important for the story?

3 What is the part played in the story by the dog Sémillante? The dog's name translates as 'bright and sprightly'. What was de Maupassant suggesting by this?

4 The widow turns an easy-going dog into a savage killer. Is the author suggesting a moral here?

5 The widow tells the dog 'Tear him! Tear him!' (line 116). The dog 'tore his throat to shreds' (line 119). Why is there so little emotion in this description? What effect does the author achieve by this?

4 Shakespeare – Macbeth

Shakespeare – *Macbeth*:
Resource Worksheets and Handouts

4a. 'What is a "Tragic Hero"?' Handout   *See page 113*

4b. 'Background to *Macbeth*' Handout   *See page 114*

4c. 'Differences between Holinshed's *Chronicles* and Shakespeare's Version' Worksheet   *See page 116*

4d. 'Time in *Macbeth*' Handout   *See page 117*

4e. 'The Macbeths: A Marriage Made in Hell' Handout   *See page 118*

4f. 'To Get you Thinking . . .' Handout   *See page 119*

4g. 'Your Coursework Essay: *Macbeth*' Handout   *See page 120*

4h. 'Coursework Essay Option 1' Handout   *See page 121*

4i. 'Coursework Essay Option 2' Handout   *See page 122*

4j. 'The Role of the Supernatural' Worksheet   *See page 124*

4k. 'Coursework Essay Options 3–8' Handout   *See page 126*

4a. WHAT IS A 'TRAGIC HERO'?

The play *Macbeth*, like *Romeo and Juliet*, is a tragedy. Romeo and Juliet, however, are not tragic heroes because their tragedy is partly due to:

✱ fate
✱ inevitability

and not to:

✱ some serious/fatal flaw of character
✱ free will.

But we *do* feel a degree of:

✱ pity (for the main characters)
✱ fear (of what is going to happen)

and

✱ a sense of tragic waste

for what the Macbeths' lives *could* have been.

So, what *does* make a tragic hero?

Macbeth himself is often referred to in these terms, whilst his wife is seen as anything between a willing agent of evil, intent on corrupting her husband, and as much a victim of circumstance as any of her husband's other 'victims'.

Aristotle (400 BC) maintained that a tragic hero:

✱ is basically a 'good' man
✱ is someone quite like ourselves
✱ has a 'fatal flaw' (or weakness) of character
✱ makes some key error of judgement
✱ falls from power, fortune or high status.

WRITING ACTIVITIES

1 Consider and make brief notes on the character of Macbeth in the light of Aristotle's comments:
   ✱ At the beginning of the play.
   ✱ At the end of Act 3.
   ✱ At the end of the play.

2 How does Macbeth change? What brings these changes about? How far is Macbeth 'responsible' for what happens in the play which bears his name? To answer these questions, you will need to consider:
   ✱ Macbeth's inner thoughts and conflicts, especially as revealed in his soliloquys and asides.
   ✱ What he actually says.
   ✱ His actions in the play.
   ✱ How he is thought of and spoken of by others.
   ✱ The influences which are brought to bear on him.
   ✱ How he responds under different pressures.

4b.   BACKGROUND TO *MACBETH*

Plot

The play *Macbeth* was written in 1606, five years after the death of Elizabeth I and the accession of James I (James VI of Scotland). Usually known as 'the Scottish play', it combines both tragedy and history. The plot is loosely based on Holinshed's *Chronicles*, published in 1577, but as usual Shakespeare made dramatic changes to:

✱ fit the Five-act Play structure
✱ engage the audience
✱ increase the ironies.

Setting

The play is set in the eleventh century, against a background of war and treachery: Sweno, King of Norway, has invaded Scotland with the aid of Ireland and the Scottish traitors Macdonwald and Cawdor. The Scottish armies, led by generals Macbeth and Banquo, have proved victorious but the air is thick with plots, counter-plots, treasons and executions. Macbeth is a 'winner' twice over: he gains the thanks of King and country and the Thanedom of Cawdor. The King is generous, but after all he and Macbeth are first cousins, sharing a common grandfather, King Malcolm:

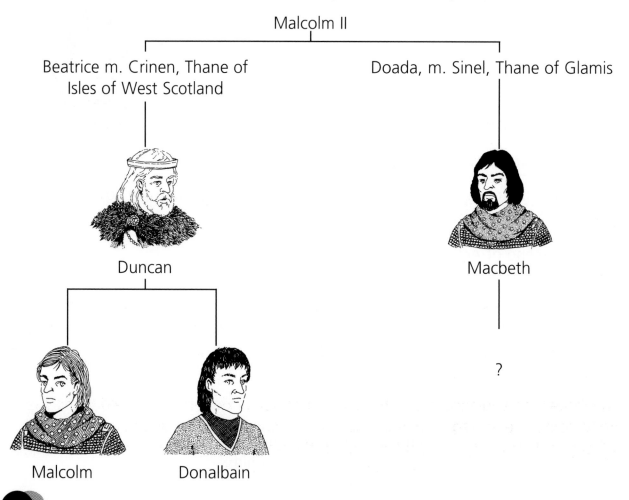

4b. BACKGROUND TO *MACBETH*

continued

Influences

James I traced his own ancestry back to Banquo, Thane of Lochquhaber, so Shakespeare had to portray him as a 'goodie' rather than as a murderous opportunist. James had also written a book about witchcraft and superstition, so this became another essential element in Shakespeare's version of events. The King not only had to be pleased, but also flattered, since Royal patronage was a great asset to an acting company. The acme of theatrical achievement was an acting company's being asked to perform at Court.

Entertainments

There were at that time three theatres on Bankside:

* the Rose
* the Swan
* the Globe.

There were all in competition with each other for:

* patronage
* good playwrights
* big audiences.

In addition, all theatres competed with other Elizabethan entertainments such as bear-baiting, bull-baiting, cock-fighting and public executions. Games such as bowls and football were also becoming popular to mass audiences; whilst the aristocracy, whose presence and money helped to popularise the theatres, also enjoyed the alternatives of hawking, hunting and jousting.

In the summer months the plague was likely to close the theatres, so the actor-managers like Henslowe (at the Rose) and Burbage (in charge of the Lord Chamberlain's Men) would lose money.

Beliefs

A largely illiterate theatre audience (apart from the gentry) enjoyed (and probably believed in) witchcraft, superstition, ghosts, fairies, hobgoblins, devils, good and bad omens and so on; and the Church itself still taught that the powers of good and evil wrestled for the possession of each individual soul.

An Elizabethan audience knew that when a character declared that he'd 'jump the life to come' (i.e. disregard any eternal consequences), he had doomed himself to tragedy in this world and to damnation in the one to come. They would, therefore, relish the 'hero's' downfall as justly deserved.

4c. DIFFERENCES BETWEEN HOLINSHED'S *CHRONICLES* AND SHAKESPEARE'S VERSION

Look at the following table and fill in the gaps. Discuss your findings, especially for the third column, with a partner.

HOLINSHED'S *CHRONICLES*	SHAKESPEARE'S VERSION	REASONS FOR THE CHANGES
Macbeth reigned for about 17 years.		
Duncan prevented Macbeth from becoming the rightful King.		
Duncan was young (as well as weak).		
Macbeth became King ten years before killing Duncan.		
Banquo helped Macbeth to kill Duncan.		
Lady Macbeth died of natural causes.		
Macbeth did not die bravely in single combat but ran away and was captured later.		

4d.   TIME IN *MACBETH*

Five-act Play

The Five-act Play is designed to give the audience a sense of rapid, almost breathtaking action: the speed of events, the haste of decisions, the 'unexpected' happenings, reversals and consequences, the movement to the inevitable dénouement.

In *Macbeth* this seems especially true: no sooner has Macbeth heard the witches proclamations that he is greeted as Thane of Cawdor by Ross; no sooner has he been called 'King hereafter', than he thinks of murdering Duncan; no sooner has Lady Macbeth received her husband's letter than she is invoking the aid of evil spirits and plotting murder.

In this play evil begets evil; choices and actions lead to other choices and actions; events snowball out of control.

Dramatic Time

'Dramatic time' clearly bears no relation to historical time: how many weeks, months or years have taken place between Act 1 and 5? We don't know and perhaps it doesn't really matter: we have witnessed transformations in characters and situations and reversals in fortune at almost break-neck speed, as though lifetimes have been contracted into five rapid Acts on the bare boards that Shakespeare said represented, 'all the world'.

4e. THE MACBETHS: A MARRIAGE MADE IN HELL?

The marriage of the Macbeths is the fertile ground into which the seed of evil falls and grows: they are first shown as an affectionate pair, who understand each other well: Macbeth addresses her as 'My dearest partner of greatness'; she analyses him as being 'too full of the milk of human kindness/To catch the nearest way.' In *her* mind, ambition and evil are linked: 'highly' and 'holily' (Act 1, Scene 5, lines 19–20) do not go together. In *his* mind, to be King is 'but fantastical' and is best left to 'chance'. Like many long-married people, the Macbeths know each other's thoughts without actually needing to speak, especially on important matters, and communicate almost in 'code', for example, 'this business', (Macbeth), 'our great quell' (Lady Macbeth), both referring to the proposed murder of Duncan.

They make, initially, a good murderous team: as in all murder fiction the unholy trinity of

* motive
* means
* opportunity

come together, with the unexpected announcement of Duncan's visit. They are leader and accomplice, but who is who? Remember that while Macbeth goes on to be a serial killer, Lady Macbeth goes mad and commits suicide . . .

WRITING ACTIVITIES

1 In pairs, look again at Act 1, Scenes 5 and 7. Discuss and make brief notes on the balance of power in the Macbeths' marriage. Who seems the stronger and why?

2 How accurate does Lady Macbeth's analysis of her husband's character prove to be?

3 Why does Lady Macbeth invoke supernatural aid?

4 Why does Macbeth decide, 'We will proceed no further in this business' (Act 1, Scene 7, line 32)? **List his reasons**.

5 How does Lady Macbeth persuade him to change his mind? **List her arguments**.

6 Why does Macbeth have hallucinations before the murder?

7 Why does Lady Macbeth have a stiff drink at the beginning of Act 2, Scene 2? What does this tell us about her?

8 Who seems the steadier and more 'together' after the murder?

9 What are Macbeth's feelings about the murder, up to the end of Act 2, Scene 2?

10 How does their marriage change later?

11 How does Macbeth react to the news of Lady Macbeth's death in Act 5, Scene 5?

4f. TO GET YOU THINKING . . .

SPEAKING & LISTENING

Before you start your coursework essay, here are several Speaking and Listening activities to stimulate your thoughts:

1 Hot-seat the following characters in turn and question them about what they did, felt or knew at different times in the play:

* Duncan (up to Act 2, Scene 2)
* Banquo (up to Act 3, Scene 3)
* Macduff
* Malcolm
* Lady Macbeth
* Ross
* First Murderer.

2 Look at this mind-map for the character of Macbeth, and discuss with a partner how much each person or aspect influences him at different points in the play.

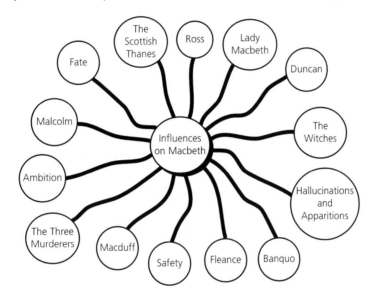

3 How important is the supernatural and its various manifestations in the play? Make a list of these manifestations, then with partner discuss their importance, especially for an Elizabethan audience.

4 On a more personal level, you might like to discuss in pairs or threes:

* How far would you be prepared to go to further an ambition, or to realise a dream?

* Would you ever 'aid and abet' a lover or close friend to achieve a goal, even if it meant breaking the law?

* How would you feel about the possible consequences if you were found out?

* Is there *anything* for which you would risk *everything*?

* Would you fear 'justice here', more than in 'the life to come'?

4g. YOUR COURSEWORK ESSAY: *MACBETH*

It is important to show good knowledge of vital Acts and Scenes that:

- **further the plot**
- **reveal characters' motives, thoughts, actions**
- **develop main themes, e.g. revenge, ambition**
- **contain vital speeches.**

Ten 'Quick Tips' for a Successful Essay

1 PLAN your essay carefully before you start.

2 PICK OUT the quotations you intend to use *and* ...

3 ... NOTE where they occur in the play.

4 MAKE your points *simply* and *clearly*.

5 BUILD UP your argument logically, so that it makes complete sense.

6 WRITE clear opening and concluding paragraphs.

7 REFER to the *whole* play, not just a part of it.

8 However, DWELL more closely on the parts directly relevant to your essay.

9 WEAVE suitable quotations into your own sentences (e.g. "Even before Macbeth enters, his reputation as 'Bellona's bridegroom' precedes him, so the audience know he is a war hero ...").

10 CHECK it over thoroughly for mistakes *before* handing it in!

COURSEWORK ESSAY OPTION 1

4h.

Essay Option 1:

> At the start they are 'brave Macbeth' and 'kind hostess', but by the end they are, 'this dead butcher and his fiend-like Queen'. How has this come about and is Malcolm's description justified?

Preparation

✱ You will need to consider, and make notes on a number of issues, including:

▶ Macbeth's military reputation at the beginning of the play and again as he prepares to meet Malcolm's army (and Macduff) in Act 5.

▶ The multiple influences on Macbeth in Acts 1 and 2, especially his military reputation at the beginning of the play and again as he prepares to meet the witches and Lady Macbeth.

▶ His 'slide' into evil and rapid change from reluctant murderer to determined serial killer.

▶ His major soliloquys which reveal his conflicts and inner changes.

▶ His increasing, irrational reliance on supernatural aid.

▶ Lady Macbeth's early strength, organisational and social skills up to Act 3, Scene 4.

▶ Her mental decline in Act 4 and suicide in Act 5.

▶ The nature of the Macbeths' marriage and how it changes during the play.

Now you have done all the preparation, you should be ready to start the first draft of your essay.

When your first draft is complete:

✱ Check it over for mistakes, e.g. punctuation, spelling, paragraphing.
✱ See that it *makes complete sense*.
✱ Put in anything you have left out.
✱ Make sure your arguments are clear.

THEN:

✱ Do your *second draft*.
✱ Check it again, as above.
✱ If you are happy with it, hand it in!

4i. COURSEWORK ESSAY OPTION 2

Essay Option 2:

> What role is played by the supernatural in 'Macbeth' and what problems are there in presenting it to a sophisticated, modern audience with quite different cultural attitudes?

Preparation

Notice that this is an essay with two distinct parts, although they are clearly related to each other.

✱ **Firstly**, the role of the supernatural in the play should include references to:

- ▶ the three witches

- ▶ Lady Macbeth invoking the aid of evil spirits

- ▶ the incitement to murder

- ▶ Macbeth's hallucinations (the dagger, voices, and so on)

- ▶ Banquo's ghost

- ▶ turmoils in the natural world which 'mirror' the unnatural deeds of the Macbeths, (for example, Act 2, Scene 4)

- ▶ the Apparitions and 'dumb show' of kings in Act 4, Scene 1

- ▶ the playing-out of the second set of prophecies in Act 5.

✱ **And**:

- ▶ the effects produced by these things on major and minor characters alike

- ▶ how the 'action' of the play is advanced by them

- ▶ their effects on the audience.

To gather all the relevant information for this part of the essay question, complete the table on 4j. 'The Role of the Supernatural' (see pages 124–25).

4i. **COURSEWORK ESSAY OPTION 2**

continued

When you have completed the table, you will have the basic information you need to answer the first part of the essay question.

✱ **Secondly**, (**a**) think about and make notes on the following questions:

▶ What *are* the problems in presenting the supernatural to a sophisticated modern audience?

▶ What problems have you and your friends encountered with the supernatural aspects of the play?

▶ Does it matter that most people no longer believe in ghosts, devils and omens?

▶ Does it matter that many people no longer believe in evil, as such?

▶ Does it matter that many no longer believe in life or punishment after death?

(**b**) Think about how modern directors of stage or film versions portray these features of the play. What presentational devices do they use? If you have seen one or more versions of the play, how were the supernatural aspects conveyed? Were they effective? Refer to them in your answer.

▶ **Do** modern audiences 'suspend their disbelief' in the supernatural in order to enjoy the play?

▶ **Do** they make an effort of historical imagination to try to understand how real these beliefs were to an Elizabethan audience?

▶ **Can** they still experience real pity and fear for the characters?

▶ **Does** the play still have enough that is important to say to a modern audience who think very differently?

▶ If **you** were directing a student version of *Macbeth*, how would you try to engage the audience in the supernatural aspects of the play?

Now you have done all the preparation, you should be ready to start the first draft of your essay.

When your first draft is complete:
✱ Check it over for mistakes, e.g. punctuation, spelling, paragraphing.
✱ Ensure that it makes complete sense.
✱ Add in anything you have left out.
✱ Make sure your arguments are clear.

THEN:
✱ Do your second draft.
✱ Check it again, as above.
✱ If you are happy with it, hand it in!

4j. **THE ROLE OF THE SUPERNATURAL**

ACT, SCENE	MANIFESTATION	DRAMATIC EFFECTS PRODUCED	OUTCOMES
Act 1 Scene 1	The three witches on the moor.	Sets scene for emergence of evil.	Audience aware of 'plot' by witches against Macbeth.
Act 1 Scene 3			
Act 1 Scene 5			
Act 2 Scene 1			
Act 2 Scene 2			
Act 2 Scene 3			
Act 2 Scene 4			

4j. THE ROLE OF THE SUPERNATURAL

continued

ACT	MANIFESTATION	DRAMATIC EFFECTS PRODUCED	OUTCOMES
Act 3 Scene 4			
Act 3 Scene 5			
Act 4 Scene 1			
Act 5 Scene 3			
Act 5 Scene 4			
Act 5 Scene 5			
Act 5 Scene 7			

4k. **COURSEWORK ESSAY OPTIONS 3–8**

3 Compare the presentation of *either* Macbeth *or* Lady Macbeth in a stage or film version you have seen with your own view of the character formed from reading the play.

4 Is Macbeth a totally evil man?

5 What is the importance of the natural world in *Macbeth*? In your answer, consider:

* animals and birds

* seasons and times of day

* their symbolic importance.

6 Examine the characters of *two* of the following and their contributions to the play:

* Banquo

* Lady Macbeth

* Malcolm

* Macduff.

7 What does *Macbeth* tell us about kingship and what makes a good king?

In your answer, consider:

* Duncan

* Macbeth

* Malcolm

* Edward the Confessor (See Act 4, Scene 3).

8 Explore the development of Macbeth's character, looking closely at his use of language and imagery. At which different points in the play does he alienate the audience's sympathy, and why?

Whichever essay you choose, use a similar preparation process to those outlined for the first two essay options. (See 4h. 'Coursework Essay Option 1' and 4i. 'Coursework Essay Option 2'.) Be prepared to spend time and effort on it and you will succeed.

⑤ Media

The Specifications

GCSE English for Edexcel Student's Book concentrates on the Media examination, according to **Edexcel Syllabus A**, the assessment criteria for which is as follows:

Assessment Objectives
Grade C

* Students are required to give personal and critical responses to literary texts which show understanding of the ways in which meaning is conveyed.

* They should refer to aspects of language, structure and themes to support their views.

Grade A*

* Students are expected to make cogent and critical responses to texts in which they explore and evaluate alternative and original interpretations.

* They should show flair and precision in developing ideas with reference to structure and presentation.

* Students must also make subtle and discriminating comparisons within and between texts.

However, if you are taking **Edexcel Syllabus B** coursework option, the following assessment criteria are followed:

Assessment Objectives
Grade C

* Students should show insight when examining:
  ▶ the nature of material, its implications and contemporary relevance
  ▶ distinctive features of style, structure and presentation
  ▶ how presentational devices, visual images and language are used to achieve a variety of effects on the audience or reader.

Grade A*

* Students are expected to show originality of analysis and interpretation when evaluating:
  ▶ the distinctive media and social context and significance of the material
  ▶ the defining achievements within the medium or genre
  ▶ patterns and details of language, presentational devices and visual images compared with other media.

It can be seen from the above assessment criteria that the work in the Student's Book on presentational devices, visual images and language is an essential part of the course.

Media: Resource Worksheets, Handouts and OHTs

Newspapers

5a. **'Newspaper Terms' Handout:** students may find a photocopy of these terms useful when they do the work on newspapers set on pages 154–172 of the Student's Book.

5b. **'Headlines' Handout:** this is a photocopiable resource for students, providing extra reinforcement of the work on headlines set on pages 155–157 of the Student's Book.

5c. **'The Inverted Pyramid' Handout:** this is a photocopiable resource that gives a detailed explanation of the inverted pyramid style of writing (extending the example on page 163 of the Student's Book), and includes practice at writing a news story in the inverted pyramid style.

5d. **'Bully Dads – A New Angle' Handout:** this editorial from the *Daily Express* adds a new angle to the concept of 'Bully Dads' introduced with the article and questions on pages 157–159 of the Student's Book.
A **Higher Tier essay** is set which requires use of both the original article and the new information from the editorial.

5e. **'A Dramatic Event' Handout:** this photocopiable resource is an extension exercise to the newspaper article and questions on pages 165–167 of the Student's Book. Two letters written to the *Daily Telegraph* following the rescue of the deer give different points of view to the newspaper article which appears in the Student's Book.
A **Higher Tier essay** is set involving the additional information from these two letters. A debate is also set as a possibility for Oral Coursework. Page 155 of Unit 6 also provides supportive teacher's notes on how to 'organise a formal debate'.

5f. **'Fact and Opinion – Part 1' Worksheet:** in the Media Texts examination (English B 1204), students are required to 'distinguish between fact and opinion and evaluate how information is presented'. Consequently, a photocopiable worksheet is included to reinforce the work on pages 168–171 of the Student's Book, along with **5g. 'Fact and Opinion – Part 2' Worksheet**, an additional photocopiable worksheet for students doing the Coursework essay on pages 187–190 of the Student's Book.

5h. **'The World' OHT:** this OHT contains a complete version of the table on page 169 of the Student's Book. Show this version to the class once they have completed their own tables and ask them to add in any details that they might have missed.

5i. **'Housebound at Sea' Handout:** this photocopiable resource contains a newspaper article which contrasts in attitude with 'Loaded-on-Sea', the article on page 170 of the Student's Book.
A **Higher Tier essay** is set which requires use of both these newspaper articles.

5j. **'A Mockery of Justice – Part 1' Worksheet:** this photocopiable resource contains a chart to help students look carefully at the article on Mr Dorrington on page 172 of the Student's Book, prior to writing the Exam Practice essay.

5k. **'A Mockery of Justice – Part 2' OHT:** this is an OHT which demonstrates the way in which the newspaper article, 'A Mockery of Justice', is written: the layout and design, photographs, language and the content. This is to help the student to answer the question in the way required in the examination.

Leaflets

5l. **'Comparison of Leaflets' Worksheet:** this photocopiable worksheet contains a chart that may be used in order to analyse the four leaflets on pages 176–180 of the Student's Book.

Magazines

5m. **'Travel Now and in the Future' OHT:** this OHT contains a mind-map showing the comparisons in writing styles, layout and design, and so on, between the two magazine articles on pages 184 and 185 of the Student's Book. This is to help the students in writing the Exam Practice essay on page 186 of the Student's Book – and will also show them a method for comparing both newspaper and magazine articles when tackling the examination.

Coursework

5n. **'Broadsheet/Tabloid Comparison' OHT:** this OHT contains a completed version of the table on page 190 of the Student's Book. Show this version to the class once they have completed their own tables and ask them to add in any details that they might have missed.

5o. **'A Mockery of Justice Coursework' Handout:** this resource consists of two further newspaper articles from *The Times* and the *Daily Mirror* covering the news story of the Dorrington case on page 172 of the Student's Book, for use in writing a comparison coursework essay.

Study of TV

It is suggested that the student compare two or three soap operas over the course of a week. It might be helpful if the teacher were to video these and show them to the class, if it becomes a whole class project – or that the student undertake to watch the chosen 'soaps' at home, if he or she is doing this project on an individual basis.

Creating a Leaflet

Following the work on leaflets, a foundation level coursework piece could be designing a leaflet on the subject of the student's choice. The student would also have to write an assessment of the leaflet, showing that he or she understood exactly the purpose of the features of the leaflet, and why he or she thought it would be successful.

5a. NEWSPAPER TERMS

Artwork:	all illustrations, charts, maps, cartoons that accompany the copy.
Banner:	the front page headline extending across a full page.
Baron:	a newspaper proprietor.
Break:	the moment when a news story emerges.
Breaker:	any device (such as a crosshead) that breaks up text on a page.
By-line:	the text giving the name of the reporter who has written the story.
Caption:	the words that accompany any picture or artwork.
Centre-spread:	the copy and pictures running over the middle two pages of a newspaper.
Classified:	small advertisements classified by subject and without any illustration.
Column:	vertical section of article appearing on page.
Copy:	the editorial material.
Crop:	the action of cutting a picture.
Crosshead:	a small heading within the body of text, usually in a larger font size.
Cut-out:	an illustration with the background 'cut out' so that the image appears on a white background.
Deck:	a unit of headline.
Diary columns:	1) gossip column. 2) day-to-day personal column.
Display ads:	large advertisements with illustrations on editorial pages.
Downpage:	the name given to a story appearing in bottom half of a page.
Drop cap:	a capital letter at the start of a paragraph taking up more than one line of text.
Editorial:	1) all non-advertising copy. 2) a column in which the newspaper expresses its own views on a topic.
Exclusive:	a story supposedly solely carried by one newspaper.
Eye-witness account:	a news story for which a reporter has been at an event, and is therefore able to give his or her own personal account.
Feature:	as distinct from news story. Tends to be longer, containing more information and including the reporter's own opinion.
Filler:	a short story, usually made up of one or two paragraphs to fill space when a long story runs short.
Hamper:	a story displayed horizontally at the top of a page.
Hard news:	news focusing on 5 Ws, factual details and little description or comment.
Human interest story:	a story focusing on success, failure, tragedy, emotional and sexual history and so on.
In-depth reporting:	covering events or issues in depth.
Layout:	the design of the page.
Lead:	the main story on a page. On the front page it is sometimes called the 'splash'.
Masthead:	the newspaper's title on the front page.
Mug shot:	a photograph just showing a person's face and sometimes shoulders.
Punchline:	the main point of the story.
Running story:	a story that develops over a number of editions or days.
Soft news:	a light news story that can be more colourful or witty than hard news.
Strap/strapline:	a headline in smaller type appearing over deck.
Tots:	an abbreviation for 'Triumph over tragedy story': popular human interest genre.

5b. HEADLINES

Airport chaos as flight control system crashes

Flight chaos as air traffic computer crashes again

Captain Blunder: I had flu

Captain's £6m blunder

Navy captain made £6m error

ACTIVITIES

1 In pairs, discuss the above headlines, which are about the same story but from different newspapers. Decide which headline you think is best, and why.

2 In pairs, write eye-catching headlines about well-known celebrities, soap operas or events, such as: 'EastEnders Axed', 'Charles Kidnapped' or 'Michael Owen Mugged'.

EXTENSION WORK

3 In pairs and using the rules on page 155 of the Student's Book, re-write the following headlines:
a) 'Game is Won in Last Minute'
b) 'Student Receives Two Honours'
c) 'Meeting of Student Council'
d) 'Many Hundreds of School Magazines Sold Out'
e) 'There are Sixteen New Students at Heathside School'.

131

5c. **THE INVERTED PYRAMID**

Paragraphs break up writing into smaller, more manageable sections. In newspapers, the reporter writes in a lively, fast-paced style that is achieved by writing in short paragraphs.

On page 163 of the Student's Book you were asked to look at the first paragraph of a newspaper article entitled 'Police dog bites off part of boy's ear', which included 3 of the 5 possible Ws. In the table below, are the four following paragraphs of the newspaper article that include both Details and Lesser Details about the incident:

Paragraph 2 (details) tells why the boy was attacked by dog.	An investigation has been launched into the incident which occurred after police were called to a street fight in Brighton involving about 20 people, some armed with bottles and knives, in the early hours of Saturday. The boy, who has not been named, was one of two teenagers who attempted to flee the scene as police arrived. A police dog handler told the boys to stop: one did but the other kept running until tackled by a six-year-old German shepherd dog.
Paragraph 3 (more details) gives further information about the incident.	A 15-year-old boy was later charged with affray and being in possession of a bladed weapon. A police spokesman said a subsequent search had uncovered another weapon at the scene.
Paragraph 4 (lesser details) gives new developments regarding the dog and the boy's ear.	The dog's temperament was being assessed by experts yesterday. If it is considered to be unsuitable for its role, it could be put down. Inspector Dave Stringer, of Sussex Police, said that after the boy had been injured, paramedics were called and police found the missing ear segment in the street.
Paragraph 5 (more lesser details) gives information about the boy's present condition, bringing the story up to date.	The boy was transferred from the Royal Sussex Hospital in Brighton to the Queen Victoria Hospital, East Grinstead, where surgeons re-attached the lower part of the ear. He was in a satisfactory condition yesterday.

THE INVERTED PYRAMID

5c.

continued

Writing in short paragraphs makes the story easy to read – as well as making it possible for the editor to cut the story short at any point without losing the sense of the piece.

WRITING ACTIVITIES

1 Using the inverted pyramid style, write up the following news story:

* Who ⟶ runaway teenager

* When ⟶ three days ago

* What ⟶ left home in early hours of morning

* Why ⟶ quarrel with parents.

This is the basis of your first paragraph.

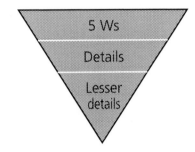

2 Now, write three further paragraphs for the news story, including more details, then lesser details, following the example given in the table.

5d. **'BULLY DADS' – A NEW ANGLE**

Shame of hooligan dads

Youth soccer is being blighted by fanatical fathers who bully their sons, scream abuse at referees and encourage children of six and seven to commit fouls and dive for penalties, according to a report by the Football Association. Games regularly erupt into violence as a result and boys leave the field in tears, vowing never to play again.

It is time these soccer dads grew up and stopped ruining sport for their own, and other people's, sons.

They should remember that football, particularly when played by children, is only a game.

 EXAM PRACTICE ESSAYS

Read the above editorial from the *Daily Express*, which adds a new angle to the concept of 'Bully Dads'.

Together with the article and questions on page 158 of the Student's Book, use this editorial to answer the following essay question:

Higher Tier Essay

'Analyse the use of both fact and opinion in the article and the editorial and their persuasive intentions.'

Using the information given, you should remember to include the following:

✱ the content of both texts.

✱ the use of headlines

✱ the use of photographs and layout

✱ the use of language

✱ your own opinion.

5e. A DRAMATIC EVENT

The following letters to the editor add a different dimension to the story of 'The Rescue of the Deer'. Read the letters and then try the speaking and listening activity and essay question set below.

Taking a dip

SIR – What satisfaction the winching up a cliff face of a deer from a Cornish cove must have brought to the coast-guard, the RNLI, the RSPCA and a veterinary practice (report, April 23). The merits of this full-scale rescue from the sea could be questioned on grounds of animal welfare, as the vet who finally tranquillised the animal commented: 'It turned out to be a very good swimmer.'

Indeed so. Deer are and, if left to its own resources, this mature roebuck, obviously in good body condition, would almost certainly have swum to the nearest landfall had it not been shepherded out of the water and then sedated by injection before being hooded, netted and harnessed up the cliff, driven to woods far from the coast and released. If the stress does not kill it, the embarrassment might.

James Darley, Aston Clinton, Bucks.

Better to be a Deer

SIR – I am inclined to agree with James Darley (letter April 25) regarding the resources used to rescue a deer. Eight weeks ago, I broke both my leg bones below the knee in a sledging accident near home. I lay immobile in the snow and biting cold wind at the bottom of a fairly steep hill for nearly an hour awaiting rescue.

An ambulance arrived with two crew, who would not carry me up the hill for safety reasons. The air ambulance was summoned, but would not respond due to lack of funds (it had already been out that day). So I then had to wait a further 45 minutes for another ambulance so that there were four staff to assist. I am not complaining about my rescue, but perhaps I should have jumped off a cliff instead of a sledge.

Alastair McFarlane, Terrington, N. Yorks.

SPEAKING & LISTENING

Oral coursework

Have a whole-class debate on the motion that: 'This House considers that we should care more for humans than for animals'.

EXAM PRACTICE ESSAY

Higher Tier Essay

Read the newspaper article on page 165 of the Student's Book and then the two letters from James Darley and Alastair McFarlane above. What impression does the article give of the rescue of the deer and what opinion does it convey? What opinion do the letters give of the rescue of the deer and what other opinions are given?

Now, write an essay entitled: 'We treat animals with more humanity than we do humans.'

Your essay should show the methods used to present the information and include:
* the use of headlines and captions
* the use of photographs
* the language and content
* your own response to the article and letters.

5f. FACT AND OPINION – PART 1

Complete the chart below, ticking the relevant box if you think the sentence is a fact or an opinion. Think carefully before you decide, as it is often more difficult than you might think.

SENTENCE	FACT	OPINION
1 That's a nice dress you're wearing.		
2 The sun is shining today.		
3 David Beckham is the best footballer in the world.		
4 I think that shopping is always fun.		
5 The Millennium Dome was a disaster.		
6 The Millennium Dome party was a wonderful start to the twenty-first century.		
7 An elephant has very thick skin.		
8 My favourite dog is a Labrador.		
9 A black cat brings you luck.		
10 Trees have green leaves.		

It is a fact that David Beckham is the best footballer in the world.

5g. FACT AND OPINION – PART 2

FACT AND OPINION – COURSEWORK ESSAY

Read the two articles on the Milan plane crash carefully and then fill in the blank spaces in the table with any relevant facts or opinions, where possible.

	THE TIMES		DAILY EXPRESS	
Paragraph	**Fact**	**Opinion**	**Fact**	**Opinion**
Paragraph 1		Stock markets and politicians . . . missed a beat last night	A plane smashed into a Milan sky-scraper yesterday	
Paragraph 2	President Bush was informed immediately		One woman leapt to her death	
Paragraph 3	Reports said that five people had died			'Everybody feared it was another terrorist attack.'
Paragraph 4	. . . fire broke out on two floors of the 417ft Pirelli Tower			. . . We suddenly realised that it was something similar to the World Trade towers
Paragraph 5		the . . . tower, which symbolises the city	67-year-old pilot Luigi Fasulo . . . had put out a distress call saying his plane's electrical system had failed.	
Paragraph 6	. . . the pilot . . . had sent out a distress call at 17.50, just before the crash			From the information in our possession, we believe it to have been an accident.

5h.

THE WORLD

QUESTIONS	RESPONSES
Where is The World presently docked?	Tatty junk yard at Greenwich, South East London
What are the facts given about the size of the ship?	holds 110 apartments 648 ft long
What are the facts given about the costs of buying an apartment on The World?	You need to be 'mega-rich' to be able to afford an apartment on The World. A small apartment costs £1.5 million. A large penthouse apartment costs £7 million.
How many and what kind of rooms do the apartments have?	We are told that a small apartment has 1 bedroom. A large penthouse apartment has 3 bedrooms and 3 marble bathrooms. A sitting room is not mentioned, neither is a kitchen.
What sports and other activities are catered for?	tennis, swimming, jogging, golf. nightclub
What opinions does the newspaper give about The World, its residents or life on it?	The millionaire residents will cruise the seven seas 'enjoying' an ever-changing view. 'You have to be mega-rich'. On the maiden voyage the residents 'will be getting to know their new homes.'
List five colloquial words used in the article and say what you think they add.	'Loaded-on-Sea' 'tatty' 'mega-rich'
Why did Athena Demartini move to The World?	She moved to The World because she was 'so scared' after the terrorist attacks in New York on September 11th.
What is her opinion of the ship?	'It seemed like a complete haven … I adore my apartment.'
What extra details are we given about Mr and Mrs Demartini?	They sold their flat on the 62nd floor of the Trump Tower, New York.

5i. HOUSEBOUND AT SEA

Housebound at Sea

The proud new owners of floating flats on The World, the cruise ship sailing round and round the globe, may live to regret their purchases. Their homes, costing between £1.4 million and £5 million, will *sometimes* have wonderful views – Monaco one morning, Marseilles the next. But for quite a lot of the time, it'll be just water, water everywhere and far too much time to think.

The ship may be big, as ships go, but it's still only 644 feet long – about a 10-minute stroll from prow to stern. You can break your walk with a visit to the tennis court or the art gallery but, unless you're a Sampras or a Saatchi, there'll still be a lot of hours left in the day to fill. Most of the supposed perks of life on board are things which, on land, any-body has access to – swimming pools, cin-emas and nightclubs.

After a while, once you've docked in Honolulu or Reykjavik for the twelfth year in a row, the most popular bits of the ship are bound to be the bar and the chapel. Yachts suddenly lose their glamour when you think of them as floating caravans. The World sounds a bit like a floating stretch limousine, for ever doomed to wander the seven seas, blessed with a boot full of champagne but damned with doors that don't unlock.

EXAM PRACTICE ESSAY

Higher Tier Essay

Read the short article above and, in conjunction with the newspaper article, 'Loaded-at-Sea' on page 170 of the Student's Book, answer the following question:

'What impression do these articles give of life on The World? Would you like to live there or not?'

In your answer you should mention:

* the content of the articles

* the use of headlines

* the use of photographs

* the use of language

* any other features of layout and design that you notice.

5j. A MOCKERY OF JUSTICE – PART 1

Read the article on page 172 of the Student's Book. Now fill in the answers to the questions in the table below using the information from the article to help you.

	THE DAILY MAIL
1 How is Mr Dorrington described?	loving father Roger Dorrington
2 How old is he?	
3 What is his job?	
4 What is the name of the drugs dealer? How old is he?	
5 What does Mr Dorrington find Mr White doing? Where was he?	
6 How is his anger described?	
7 How much compensation does the Judge order Mr. Dorrington to pay?	
8 How much community service is he asked to do?	
9 With whom will he be expected to do his community service?	
10 How old were the Dorrrington boys, Nick and Joseph, when they first took drugs?	
11 What does Mr Dorrington say about his two sons now?	
12 Where are they now living?	
13 What are they doing?	
14 Write down the story using Mr Dorrington's own words.	
15 What did his MP say about the judgement?	

5k. **'A MOCKERY OF JUSTICE' – PART 2**

Using 'A Mockery of Justice' as an example, this OHT shows the key features of a newspaper article that you should consider when answering an exam question.

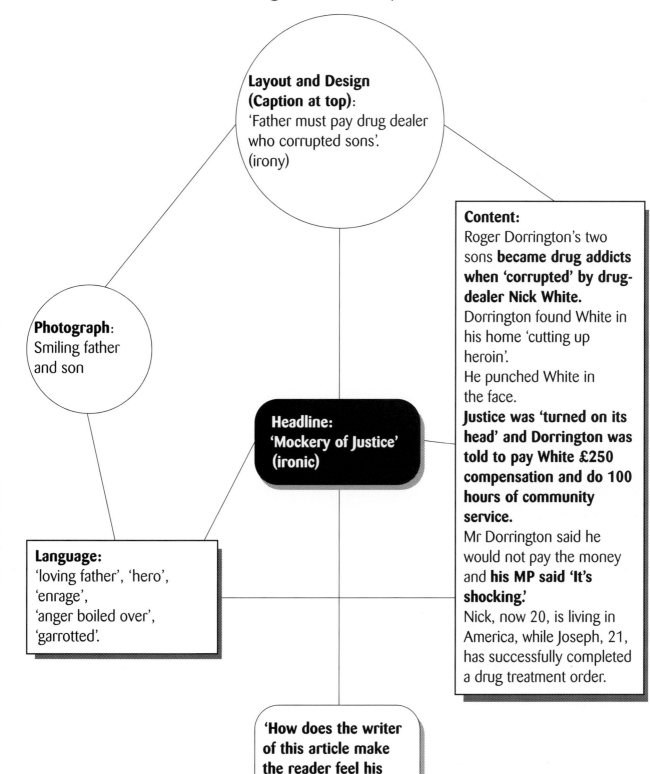

Layout and Design (Caption at top):
'Father must pay drug dealer who corrupted sons'.
(irony)

Photograph:
Smiling father and son

Headline:
'Mockery of Justice'
(ironic)

Language:
'loving father', 'hero',
'enrage',
'anger boiled over',
'garrotted'.

Content:
Roger Dorrington's two sons **became drug addicts when 'corrupted' by drug-dealer Nick White.**
Dorrington found White in his home 'cutting up heroin'.
He punched White in the face.
Justice was 'turned on its head' and Dorrington was told to pay White £250 compensation and do 100 hours of community service.
Mr Dorrington said he would not pay the money and **his MP said 'It's shocking.'**
Nick, now 20, is living in America, while Joseph, 21, has successfully completed a drug treatment order.

'How does the writer of this article make the reader feel his sense of outrage?'

5l.   COMPARISON OF LEAFLETS

Write your answers in detail in the chart below, supporting your answers with information from the leaflets on pages 176–179 of the Student's Book.

	LEAFLET	LEAFLET ....
What makes the leaflet EITHER a) clear and easy to understand? OR b) confused and difficult to understand?		
Are the colours appropriate to the subject?		
Are the headlines zappy – attracting attention?		
Is the language appropriate for the subject?		
Does the use of language attract attention through unusual words?		
Are the directions clear (for example, telephone number, address, instructions)?		
Does the leaflet give you information or is it trying to sell a product?		
What do the photographs or drawings add to the leaflet? Are they useful or attractive, or both?		
Describe the layout. Is it well-designed – or could the leaflet be more clearly laid out?		

5m. TRAVEL NOW AND IN THE FUTURE

SoloTrek Flying Vehicle

Layout and Design: SoloTrek article – text in rectangular shape with photograph of SoloTrek in the corner.

Photograph: shows man strapped on to the SoloTrek Flying Vehicle. It helps our understanding of the vehicle.

Compare the two articles on the 'SoloTrek Flying Vehicle' and the MG TF. Consider their presentation, language and tone. Which do you think is the most effective, and why?

Headlines: above the article and a caption under the photograph. The short, snappy headline is eye-catching. ('need a lift . . . commuting starts to take off').

Language: lively opening 'a joke' followed by factual detail 'altitude of 24 inches . . . for 19 seconds.'
Scientific: 'Powered by a paraffin-fuelled piston engine . . . primarily designed for military applications.'
Use of direct quotation: will 'take off . . . like a helicopter'. (makes idea more believable)

MG TF

Layout and Design: MG TF article – text in rectangular shape. No photograph, just a boxed insert with facts.

No photograph: this would have enhanced the article – showing through colour and shape the car's 'sexy' look.

Headlines: these are above the article. Again, eye-catching with 'Hey, good-looking' in large, bold letters. Using the word 'wolf-whistling' is an attention-grabbing caption.

Language: conversational and lighthearted: 'like going on a first date', a lively comparison, which is instantly interesting.
Uses more **comparisons: a)** effect of car on builders and 'me . . . in my pyjamas'; **b)** car and 'supermodel'; **c)** interior and 'nasty pair of Y-fronts'.
Use of direct quotation: 'a nice snappy little motor'.

143

5n. BROADSHEET/TABLOID COMPARISON

FRONT PAGE	THE TIMES	DAILY EXPRESS
size of photographs	third of page	two-thirds of page
size of headlines	large/medium	medium
text of headlines	'My God, it's like New York all over again'	'Five killed as plane flies into packed skyscraper'
amount of text in story	one-third photograph two-thirds text	photograph — just over half text — just under half
summary of story	Stock markets 'missed a beat' when 'a light aircraft crashed into Milan's tallest building'. Italian Prime Minster convened emergency meeting fearing attack similar to September 11 attack in US. crash believed to be an accident. Report that 5 people, including the pilot, had died. Dozens injured. Pilot had been flying to Milan from Switzerland, had reported problem with plane's undercarriage before crashing into tower.	Plane smashed into Milan skyscraper. 5 killed, scores injured. Light aircraft ploughed into 25th floor of Italy's Pirelli Tower. 'Everybody feared it was another terrorist attack.' The plane's electrical system had failed; it was believed to be 'an accident'.
words and phrases used to describe accident	'missed a beat' 'crashed' 'suicide attack' 'convened emergency meeting' 'stock markets … dropped sharply' 'leapt to her death' 'covered in blood' 'dozens were injured' 'smoke was rising' 'gash in its side' 'ploughing into the 30-storey tower'	'Plane smashed' 'chilling memories' 'woman leapt to her death' 'black smoke billowed' 'aircraft ploughed' 'terrified eye-witness' 'world put on alert'
number of people giving first-person accounts	Police Officer Celerissimo De Simone	Two people: Persivale Matteo Maurizio Sala

5n.

BROADSHEET/TABLOID COMPARISON

continued

FRONT PAGE	THE TIMES	DAILY EXPRESS
facts	'light aircraft crashed into Milan's tallest building' Silvio Berlusconi, the Italian Prime Minister, convened an emergency defence and security meeting' 'President Bush was informed immediately' 'stock markets in New York and Frankfurt dropped sharply' 'fire broke out on two floors of the 417ft Pirelli Tower, which is five miles from the airport where the pilot had been heading'. 'The pilot of the Rockwell Commander single-engined plane flying to Milan from Locarno in Switzerland had sent a last-minute SOS message reporting problems with plane's undercarriage'. '30-storey tower' 'Police officer Celerissimo De Simone said ... the pilot ... had sent out a distress call at 17.50, just before the crash near the city's main railway station'.	'32-storey building.' '25th floor of ... Pirelli Tower' 'propeller-driven light aircraft' 'two explosions' 'thousands of pieces of paper ... flying through the air' 'Military helicopters and jets scrambled' 'security forces ... put on alert' '67-year-old pilot' 'plane's electrical system had failed'
opinions	'Stock markets and politicians missed a beat.' 'Aroused fears of a suicide attack,' 'Believed the crash was an accident.' 'My God, it's New York all over again,' said a bystander. It was believed that the pilot, distracted by problems with the undercarriage failed to notice how close he was to the building. 'The tower ... symbolises the city.'	'...killing at least five people and injuring scores.' 'Two women passers-by were believed to have been killed by falling debris.' 'Everybody feared it was another terrorist attack.' ' ... we believe it to have been an accident.'

5o. 'A MOCKERY OF JUSTICE' COURSEWORK

Using the original newspaper article about Mr Dorrington in the Student's Book, compare it with the following two articles from *The Times* and *The Mirror* to write a coursework essay entitled: 'The article on the Dorrington case I find most interesting, and why'.

As well as saying what you found most compelling in the article of your choice, you should also state why the other articles failed to grip your attention.

In your answer you must mention:

the use of banner, headlines and captions
the use of photographs
the content

the use of language
the use of first-hand accounts
the inclusion of fact and opinion.

Court backs drug dealer attacked by victim's father

By Lewis Smith

A father has been ordered to pay compensation to a drug dealer he beat up after finding him supplying his younger son with heroin.

Roger Dorrington, a businessman in the New Forest, was ordered to pay the dealer, James White, £250 in compensation after he admitted a charge of assault.

The court was told that Dorrington had banned Mr White from his home because he had been supplying both his sons. On the day of the attack Mr White had been out buying heroin with one of them, Nicholas.

Dorrington, 48, returned to his bungalow on June 2 last year to find Mr White measuring out heroin in his bedroom. Dorrington lost his temper and attacked Mr White, of Woodgreen, Hampshire, punching him 15 times in the face. The dealer, who suffered cuts and bruises, complained to the police and Dorrington was arrested.

Mr White, 24, has not faced a drugs charge, but Dorrington was arrested for assault. At Southampton Crown Court he was also ordered to do 100 hours' community servce.

Desmond Swayne, the Conservative MP for New Forest West, was infuriated by the sentence. 'Have the courts gone mad? If it was my children, I would have garrotted him with his own intestines ... I do not know how long we can go on enduring this sort of madness,' he said.

Ann Widdecombe, the former Tory spokeswoman for home affairs, described the case as 'upside-down justice' and could not understand why Mr White had not faced charges himself. 'What the house-holder should have done was to call the police but the more guilty party was clearly the dealer,' she said.

Colin Smith, of Narcotics Anonymous, was concerned about the father's treatment. He said: 'This seems harsh. What he did was just a father's natural reaction, and paying £250 compensation is ridiculous. We all know he [White] is just going to buy more drugs.'

Dorrington said yesterday that he had no regrets and would do the same again. He said that Mr White had introduced his sons, Joseph, 21, and Nicholas, 20, to heroin when they were 15 and 14, and that he had been battling to break their addiction for six years. Mr White would not see a penny in compensation, he said and added: 'I am gutted. I just feel hard done by. This is not justice. It's been an absolute nightmare. My house has been broken into a number of times, my cheque books stolen. I've had £50,000 taken off me in the previous six years because of all this.

'James White was in my house cutting up drugs and supplying them in my bedroom. I thought I had some justification to remove him from my property.'

He was sentenced on Friday by Judge David Griffiths who said that punishment was a matter for the courts, not individuals, but that he understood, 'given the circumstances, how you lost your temper'. It was for this reason that Dorrington was sentenced to community service rather than prison.

Katherine Hunter, for the defence, told the judge: 'After six years trying to get his sons off this dreadful, dreadful drug one can perhaps understand why he did what he did.'

Both Dorrington's sons are now off heroin.

5o. 'A MOCKERY OF JUSTICE' COURSEWORK

continued

● **Dad beat up dealer who sold heroin to sons he's been trying to get off drugs for six years**

● **Now he's got to do community service ... and pay the DEALER £250 compensation**

DEFIANT: Dad Roger Dorrington, left, and former heroin addict son Joseph

IT'S MADNESS

By NIC NORTH

A father who beat up a drug dealer for trapping his sons on heroin has been ordered to pay him £250 compensation.

Fury and disbelief yesterday greeted the court decision.

Dad Roger Dorrington, who had fought for six years to wean his boys off drugs and away from supplier James White, said there was 'no justice' and vowed not to pay.

His local MP Desmond Swayne called the judgment 'madness' and added; 'If it was my children, I would have garrotted him with his own intestines.'

Mr Dorrington, a 48-year-old businessman, said White introduced his sons Nick and Joseph to drugs when they were 14 and 15.

He later banned him from their home in the New Forest hamlet of Blissford, Hants.

Last June he caught him at the bungalow, 'cutting up drugs'. He realised White and son Nick had been out buying heroin, a judge was told.

White, 24, fled and was caught by Mr Dorrington in his van outside.

The furious dad punched him in the face 15 times, causing cuts and bruises.

Mr Dorrington admitted assault causing bodily harm and was given 100 hours' community service, plus the compensation order, by Southampton Crown Court.

Judge David Griffiths told him last Friday that 'given the circumstances', he would not send him to prison.

Mr Dorrington said yesterday: 'For six years I had been trying to get my sons away from White. Yet he wasn't arrested for anything he did.

'There is no justice. I am the victim here, not James White. I feel absolutely gutted.'

He added: 'I am not paying on principle. I would rather give £1,000 to charity.

'If I did give him the money and he supplied someone with heroin and that person died, I wouldn't be able to live with myself. I do not have any regrets. I would do it all again.'

Mr Dorrington said the drugs scene had been an 'absolute nightmare' for him.

'My house has been broken into a number of times, my chequebooks stolen. I've had £50,000 taken off me in the previous six years because of all this.

'Drugs are evil. You should see the change in my boys when they come off them.'

Joseph, 21, has now successfully completed a treatment order and Nick, 20, is off drugs and living in America. MP Mr Swayne, who represents New Forest West for the Tories, called the episode a 'scandal' and will try to raise it in the Commons.

He asked: 'If you found yourself in the position of Mr Dorrington what would you have done?

'Have the courts gone made, I know we have separation between the legal branch and politicians, but I do not know how long we can go on enduring this sort of madness.'

Narcotics Anonymous said Mr Dorrington's sentence was 'harsh'.

Spokesman Colin Smith added: 'What he did was just a father's natural reaction.'

'WRITING TRIPLETS' INTRODUCTION

The Specifications

The 'Writing Triplets' are assessed by examination, as follows:

WRITING TO:	ENGLISH A (1203)	ENGLISH B (1204)
argue, persuade, advise	Papers 3F/5H	Section B
inform, explain, describe	Papers 2F/4H	Section C
analyse, review, comment	Papers 3F/5H	Section C

Assessment Objectives

1 Students are required to communicate clearly and imaginatively, using and adapting forms for different readers and purposes.

2 They need to organise their ideas into sentences, paragraphs and whole texts using a variety of linguistic and structural features.

3 They are further required to use a range of sentence structures effectively with accurate punctuation and spelling.

Many of the skills required for 'Writing to Inform, Explain and Describe, for example, will be familiar to students from work undertaken at Key Stage 3, but 'Writing to Argue and Persuade' and 'Writing to Analyse and Review' will probably be less familiar, and will therefore need more teacher guidance and cumulative student practice.

As the 'Writing Triplets' integrate a lot of oral work, you could build this up into group discussions, formal debates, pair work or even solo talks, on which oral assessments could be given. The notes on how to organise a formal debate (page 150) are a useful resource.

A range of writing skills are incorporated, such as: a speech, report, playscript, letter, argument essay, and so on.

6 Writing to Argue, Persuade, Advise

Writing to Argue: Resource Worksheets, Handouts and OHTs

These are intended to supplement the information given in the Student's Book and to be a handy resource bank for teachers.

6a. **'Drafting' Handout:** this resource is a 'reminder' handout which can be issued to students when they begin any piece of coursework so that they can use it as a check-list against which to monitor their own work.

6b. **'For and Against Capital Punishment' OHT:** this OHT relates directly to the activities undertaken in the Student's Book (pages 194–197) and gives you a ready source of reference in order to help the weaker candidates to find more arguments when they get stuck at five or six points and cannot think of any others. You can also use it as a general check-list to go through when discussing each of the main arguments with the whole class.

6c. **'Alternative Letter to the Editor' Handout:** this is a Higher Tier alternative to the simplified letter found in the Student's Book on page 198. More able students should enjoy rising to the challenge of a more complex and detailed letter, while benefiting from being able to highlight and annotate the key points within it.

Writing to Argue: Revision Questions

These six revision questions are for use at your own discretion, for example, they could be used for more able students or as homework assignments for exam practice. They cover a range of writing genre (letter, playscript, magazine article, report) for different audiences and purposes and are therefore useful revision exercises.

1 Write an article for an adult magazine, such as *Hello*, arguing either **for** or **against** teenagers having televisions in their own rooms, where they can watch anything at any time.

2 Write an article for a school magazine, arguing for the abolition of a school rule that you think is either outdated, unfair or unnecessary.

3 Write a letter to your local council arguing for more sports facilities for young people in your town or village.

4 A good Saturday job has been advertised in the local newspaper. You want to apply for it but your parents are against it, arguing that it will interfere with your studies. Structure a playscript in which you try to convince them that a job would have many benefits, apart from welcome extra money.

5 Write a speech in defence of the proposition that, 'The age of legal adulthood should be dropped from 18 to 16.'

6 Write a report to the School Council, on behalf of Year 11 pupils, arguing that they should have an improved Year 11 Common Room, with a kitchen, photocopying facilities, and a stereo system.

Writing to Argue: Teacher's Notes

Organising a Formal Debate: these following pages of Teacher's Notes give you a potted summary of the basic organisation of a formal debate, should you or the students themselves decide to hold a debate on capital punishment or a similar topic. As well as oral assessments for the main speakers, a debate gives students the opportunity to organise their thoughts, argue a case, and listen or respond to, other points of view. If you are introducing formal debating for the first time, it is a good idea to chair it yourself, then encourage the students to take on this role at a later date.

Organising a Formal Debate

1 After discussion with the class, select a topic for debate and turn this into a **Motion**, for example, 'This House believes that capital punishment should be re-introduced for premeditated murder,' or 'This House believes that homework should be abolished.'

2 Then, after the class has written the first draft of proposing and opposing speeches (you could divide the class in half for this) select four to six main speakers, to assume the following roles:

Proposer of Motion
Opposer of Motion
Proposer's Second
Opposer's Second

The roles appear in the order of speaking.

Either select two other speakers, one to sum up for each side, or ask the speakers in the role of the 'Seconds' to sum up.

3 Allow the main speakers time to practise in their teams, making sure you check that their speeches dovetail each other rather than repeat the same points in the same way.

4 Encourage the rest of the class to write three to four questions for each team when the debate is open to the floor.

5 **Order of proceedings** (you may wish to Chair the first debate yourself if debating is new to the school; if it is well-established, select an able and firm Chairperson from the students):
a) Introduce the Motion and the four to six speakers.
b) Take a straw poll of those who, at the outset, are:

For   Against   Abstaining from

"the Motion."

c) Call upon the speakers in the order given:

Proposer of Motion
Opposer of Motion

These roles have up to 9 minutes each in which to speak.

| Proposer's Second | These roles have up to 4 minutes each in |
| Opposer's Second | which to speak. |

d) Open the discussion up to the floor, allowing questions to the speakers through the Chair, or the making of personal statements from the audience.

e) If the questions and answers are lively, allow this to continue for 10–15 minutes or until all questions are exhausted.

f) Ask each team to sum up its main arguments (either the Seconds or a third team member), allowing up to 3 minutes for each side.

g) Take the real count of those:

| For | Against | Abstaining from |

"the Motion."

h) Declare the Motion either carried or defeated and thank all concerned.

The main speakers may be given oral assessments on their performances (including how they answered questions from the floor and the opposing team), as could student members of the audience who made substantial personal statements.

6a.

DRAFTING

First Draft

This is the 'rough' copy of your writing and may be partly in note form. Put all your ideas together and map out how you would like the final draft of your writing to look.

Alternatively, you may like to draw a mind-map to help you work out the main points of your essay. Use the example of a mind-map given below to help you.

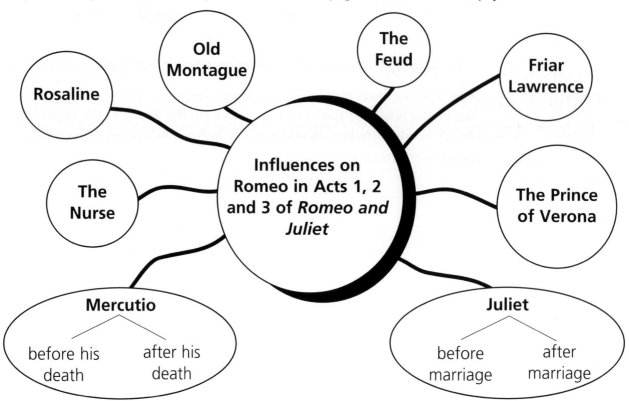

Re-drafting

Before you write a second draft, look through your first draft again keeping the following points in mind:

1 Do the paragraphs link together sensibly?
2 Have I got the paragraphs in the right order?
3 Is the meaning of my writing clear?
4 Does it sound right or do I need to change any words or phrases?
5 Is the spelling and punctuation accurate?
6 Has anything important been missed out?

Final Draft

Once you have made the necessary changes and corrections, set out your final, neat draft, including any illustrations you may be using.

6b. CAPITAL PUNISHMENT

Arguments For:

1 Others are deterred from committing murders.

2 It is a just response – a life for a life.

3 Society has a right to defend itself against violent crime.

4 The murderer knows the consequences before he commits the crime.

5 It saves money that would have been spent on keeping the criminal in prison.

6 It stops the possibility of repeated murders after 7–10-year 'life' sentences.

7 The relatives of the victims can be satisfied.

8 The public – on a referendum – would restore it.

9 Criminals would think twice before killing if their own lives were at stake.

Arguments Against:

1 'Society makes the crime, the criminal commits it.'

2 Only God has the right to give and take life. All life is sacred.

3 Killing the murderer is itself committing murder.

4 It is not helpful to react to violence with further violence.

5 The innocent might be convicted.

6 The difficulty of finding an executioner.

7 It is difficult for juries to convict fairly as doubts and moral scruples can affect the decision.

8 The criminals might be reformed and, therefore, become useful members of society.

9 The family of the criminal would suffer for crime committed by one of their members.

10 Capital punishment is not a proven deterrent.

6c. ALTERNATIVE LETTER TO THE EDITOR

The Editor,
The Times.

Sir,

Isn't it about time someone spoke up and admitted how awful today's teenagers are? There is no respect for authority, such as teachers and parents, and none for the law either (witness the rising tide of juvenile delinquency) from this generation.

Truancy rates are soaring and with them illiteracy in school leavers, along with innumeracy, bad manners, lack of punctuality and a 'don't care, don't want to care,' attitude. No wonder employers are finding it increasingly hard to fill their vacancies. In any case, many teenagers, after making little effort at school, leave without jobs or college places and expect to be kept by us, the taxpayers! Many even refuse the opportunities offered by the Y.T.S. and other government schemes.

In addition, look at the rise in football hooliganism, burglaries and muggings by the under-sixteens, drug, solvent and alcohol abuse, and the spread of Aids, to say nothing of the dramatic rise in schoolgirl pregnancies, abortions, and illegitimate births.

When is something effective going to be done to bring this generation to heel? Do we have to bring back National Service to inculcate discipline, smartness, and obedience to rules and laws, or is the Government prepared to take action to put this country back on its feet?

Why not start by making parents responsible for their children's misdemeanours by heavy fines, or imprisonment, if necessary? Children over sixteen should be responsible for their own actions and dealt with severely when they offend against society — community service is too soft an option. Action please, before it's too late!
[Name and address supplied.]

Part B: Writing to Persuade

Warm-up oral exercises are a good way to get straight into the *how* and *why* of each segment of the Writing Triplets. As well as those suggested in the Student's Book, you could get them to try to 'sell' an object to each other, such as a new type of pen, mobile phone or game-boy, then change roles and discuss the success or otherwise of the techniques of persuasion they employed. Alternatively, get them each to bring in a magazine advertisement they think is effective, and explain how or why it is so persuasive.

Writing to Persuade: Resource Handout and OHT

6d. **'Persuasive Letters' Handout:** this can be issued directly to the students as a handout for homework or exam revision. The subject of 'Litter and the Environment' remains a topical one and the assignment is a good exercise in persuasive writing.

Writing to Persuade: Revision Questions

In the same way as for 'Writing to Argue', these questions may be used at your own discretion. They cover a range of writing genre (letter, playscript, speech, magazine article) for different audiences and purposes and are therefore useful revision exercises.

1 Your friend has had an offer of interesting work abroad plus the opportunity of travelling for his or her gap year, but has also had a tempting offer from the university of his or her choice and can't decide what to do. Write a letter to *persuade* him or her to adopt one course of action or the other.

2 Write a playscript showing how you could successfully persuade your reluctant parents to let you go abroad on an unsupervised camping holiday with friends after your GCSE exams.

3 Write a speech to be given during school assembly to persuade fellow pupils to vote you on to the School Council. (Explain what you will do for them, issues you will take up, and why you are a suitable person to represent their interests.)

4 You have very noisy neighbours. Write a polite but firm letter trying to persuade them to change their behaviour.

5 Write an article for a magazine aimed at parents, trying to persuade them to allow their teenage children more independence.

6 Write a persuasive speech in favour of the Motion: 'Children should have more say in the subjects they study at school.'

6d. PERSUASIVE LETTERS

Persuasive letters can be either **informal** (to people you know) or **formal** (business letters to people you have not met). They have a quite different layout and tone. For example, in an informal or friendly letter you:

✱ may choose whether or not to put your address

✱ usually put the date

✱ may begin 'Hi John' or 'Dear John'

✱ may end with 'Best wishes', 'See you soon', 'Bye for now', 'Love from', and so on

✱ may use slang or incomplete sentences.

1 Read the following short article on the subject of 'Litter':

The Importance of Litter and the Environment ● ● ●

Litter comes in many shapes and forms. It includes waste paper, broken glass and metal cans in the street and hedgerows. It also includes illegal dumping, where items such as neglected cars, prams and mattresses are often discarded.

Litter is dirty, ugly and unhygienic – causing a threat to everyone's safety and health.

Litter has become a very important environmental issue, prompting extensive media coverage. In 1990 everyone had the opportunity to combat litter by supporting the Tidy Britain Year initiative.

When we consider the facts about litter and our environment it is clear to see that action must be taken quickly to combat the problem.

The Facts about Rubbish

● Britain produces over 60 million tonnes of rubbish each year.

● Every year over 3 million milk bottles are discarded.

● The Kings Cross fire in the London Underground, which caused 31 deaths, and the Bradford Football Stadium fire which caused 53 deaths, were partly due to litter.

PERSUASIVE LETTERS

continued

- Each week the equivalent of 4,350 spruce trees are collected from our motorway carriageways in the form of waste paper.

The Facts about our Environment

- Plastics injure and kill animals. In a survey of one river over 9 kilometres of nylon fishing line were found. In the same survey 20 entangled, injured and dead birds were found.

- A forest the size of Wales is required to provide Britain with one year's supply of paper. Only 5% of it is recycled.

The only solution to the litter problem is to change people's attitudes to the environment so that they understand the benefits of a clean and beautiful country and take responsibility for keeping it that way. This task of changing people's attitudes is not easy – these are some of the methods that are being tried:

- advertising campaigns can change attitudes by increasing awareness of the issue

- heavier fines for littering

- improving recycling facilities

- better education of children and adults

- better street cleansing.

'Litter creates more litter – once an area has become littered, people treat it like a public tip.

We must help prevent litter and change the facts.' (Common Entrance Board, 1990)

2 Now imagine that you have a friend who is a real litter-bug showing no concern whatever for the environment. Using the information in the article above and any other ideas of your own, write your friend an informal letter, trying to persuade him or her to change his or her attitudes and behaviour.

Part B: Writing to Advise

This section has, as yet, no sample questions on the specimen exam papers, so as broad a view of it as possible needs to be taken, such as personal, professional or practical advice.

The means deployed include oral work, letters, articles, leaflets and reports, to cover different audiences and purposes.

Writing to Advise: Revision Questions

These four revision questions are for use at your own discretion, for example they could be used for more able students or as homework assignments for exam practice. They cover a range of writing genre (playscript, report, account, advice sheet) for different audiences and purposes and are therefore useful revision exercises.

1 Prepare a report on the topic of school lunches in your school, advising the Headteacher of any changes or improvements you think should be made.

2 A new family has moved in next door, who do not know your area at all. They have asked you to advise them where 1) the basic amenities, such as shops, schools, restaurants, buses etc. are, and 2) what leisure facilities are available locally. Write a brief account of the advice you would give them.

3 Write an advice sheet on dating for boys and girls aged 12–14.

4 One of your friends has a problem with bad breath but seems unaware of it. In playscript form, structure a conversation where you *tactfully* bring up the subject and offer some advice on how to tackle it. Show your friend's reaction clearly.

7 Writing to Inform, Explain, Describe

Part A: Writing to Inform

'Writing to Inform, Explain, Describe' *ought* to be the easiest of the three 'Writing Triplets' to teach, as students have been practising these skills all their lives and during Key Stage 3 will have learnt to do it in a structured way. However, giving clear information remains a problem for many adults including the writers of manuals and 'how-to' books or articles. It is essential to build up skills and confidence through frequent practice.

Writing to Inform: Resource Handout and OHT

7a. **'Higher Tier Extension Work' Handout:** in this resource students are asked to write an information leaflet on Acrylamide based on the material given.

7b. **'Specimen Information Leaflet' OHT:** this OHT contains part of a specimen information leaflet from British Rail which should be used as an example when students attempt the Information Leaflet on **7a. 'Higher Tier Extension Work' Handout**.

Writing to Inform: Revision Questions

These six revision questions are for use at your own descretion, for example they could be used for more able students or as homework assignments for exam practice. They cover a range of writing genre (formal and informal letters, playscript, newspaper and magazine articles) for different audiences and purposes and are therefore useful revision exercises.

1 You are the parent of a child from Year 7 or 8. Write a letter to the Headmaster, informing him of a problem that your child is having (for example, being bullied, having too much homework, not enough time for lunch) and asking for help in solving it. Set it out correctly in business letter format.

2 Write the Headmaster's reply (remembering to reverse the addresses), giving suitable information about the school's policy on the issue(s), and suggesting a possible solution.

3 Write an article for a newspaper informing the readers what 16-year-old students really think about the education system many of them are about to leave.

4 Inform your parents, in playscript form, what you intend to do during your gap year. This is all news to them. Make *your* plans and *their* reactions equally clear.

5 Inform a school friend, who has been off ill for three weeks, what has been going on in their absence. Make your letter lively and chatty. Include gossip as well as facts, which you think would interest them.

6 Give helpful information to someone in Year 9 who is about to choose their GCSE options. Write it *either* as a personal letter, *or* as a short article for the school magazine.

7a. HIGHER TIER EXTENSION WORK

1 Read the following questions and answers on the latest food scare:

How serious is the latest food scare?

1. What is the problem?
Frying and baking create high levels of acrylamide – a potential cancer-causing chemical – in a wide range of food. Acrylamide was not known to occur at these levels in food prior to this research.

2. What do we know about acrylamide and its health risks?
Animal data and our understanding of its biological effects suggest acrylamide is a probable human carcinogen. It is known to cause nerve damage in humans and to impair fertility in male animals.

Practically nothing is known about its effects on humans via the diet, although scientists advise that exposure to DNA-damaging carcinogens such as acrylamide should be as low as reasonably practicable.

3. Is this a new risk?
No. Acrylamide appears to be formed in food by common cooking practices and so people are likely to have been exposed to acrylamide for some considerable time.

4. How serious a risk is acrylamide to human health?
Eating is not a completely risk-free activity, with many more immediate risks such as food poisoning from not cooking food thoroughly.

There are many other causes of cancer including lifestyle and environmental factors. Some people are more susceptible than others to particular factors.

5. Is acrylamide an immediate risk?
No. The FSA says any possible risks to human health from acrylamide in food would arise from long-term exposure.

6. Can we measure the risk to human health?
The UK Independent Committee on Carcinogenicity of Chemicals in Food, Consumer Products and the Environment (COC) does not consider it valid to calculate numbers of anticipated human cancer cases from the results of animal studies.

The COC decided that such calculations gave an impression of precision, which could not be justified from the assumptions made relating to the biological events leading to cancer and the different nature of exposure.

It advises that exposure to DNA-damaging carcinogens such as acrylamide should be as low as reason-ably practicable. Such carcinogens are not permitted to be added to food.

7. Why has it taken until now to identify its presence in food?
It was not previously known that acrylamide could or would be produced during cooking. It was uncovered as a result of a chance finding in Swedish studies and confirmed by a British study.

8. Should we be cooking our food for shorter periods to reduce our exposure to acrylamide in food?
No. All food, especially meat, should be cooked properly to destroy food-poisoning bacteria.

9. What can be done to avoid acrylamide in food?
There are no practical ways in which it can be avoided. A healthy, balanced diet, including plenty of fruit and vegetables, will help to protect against some cancers.

10. Can I still eat chips and crisps?
The FSA is not advising people to stop eating any of the foods sampled. However, as part of a balanced diet you should limit the amount of fried and fatty foods you eat, including chips and crisps.

2 Now use this material as the basis of an information leaflet giving advice to the general public, from the Food Standards Authority (FSA).

7b. SPECIMEN INFORMATION LEAFLET

Clearly set out

do

1. Be considerate to the other people who want to use the station.
2. Allow plenty of time at the station before your train is due.
3. Walk – don't run
4. Stay off the tracks
5. Keep away from the platform edge
6. Obey all signs
7. Keep a close watch on small children
8. Secure prams and pushchairs

don't!

9. Try to get on or off a moving train.
10. Ride bikes or use skateboards on the platform

Brief, note-like instructions

'Prettified' Station

Numbered Points

AMUSING PICTURES

Helpful porter

British Rail logo

Subject of leaflet

The **Railway Code**

Safety

Cover

Title echoes 'The Highway Code'

Part B: Writing to Explain

Explaining a process could be an initial whole-class writing activity, for example, explaining the best way of making a paper aeroplane. The first Writing Activity on page 212 of the Student's Book provides a structure for this whole-class writing activity. Students are asked to conduct a similar experiment in groups of four to six. Conduct the activity using the outline provided, then discuss the outcome (success or otherwise) and what can be learnt from it, either before they do their group work or afterwards.

There is ample scope here to turn some of their oral assignments into Oral Coursework Assessments.

Writing to Explain: Teacher's Notes

A useful group activity can be the Balloon Debate – it could equally well be a small boat or helicopter, and so on, but it must be in difficulty. Each student is given an identity in this balloon, such as a mother of eight, a cancer scientist, a nuclear physicist, a primary school teacher, a pop star, a social worker with a large caseload, a chat show host, and so on. Each student has to explain or argue why he or she should not be the one to be thrown out of the balloon to save the lives of the others.

Writing to Explain: Revision Questions

These six revision questions are for use at your own discretion, for example they could be used for more able students or as homework assignments for exam practice. They cover a range of tasks and topics, for example, explaining feelings, past events, family traditions, childhood memories, work experience and gap year issues.

1 Choose an event from your past that has a special significance for you. Explain what happened and your feelings about it.

2 Many families have their own traditions, which may include how they celebrate birthdays, personal successes, anniversaries or religious festivals. Explain some of your family's traditions and what they mean to you.

3 Some decisions can be difficult to make. Think back to any difficult decision you or a member of your family have had to make. Explain what the decision was and what happened as a result of it.

4 Many writers write about their childhood memories of people, places or events, and how they have been affected by these. Write about one of your own childhood memories and explain how it has affected you.

5 Explain how work experience can benefit young people still at school. Refer to your own work experience, if you have any.

6 Explain why you would or would not like to have a gap year between finishing your A Levels and starting university.

Part C: Writing to Describe

The emphasis in this part of the 'Writing Triplet' is on people, places and things, and the use of adjectives, verbs, metaphors and similes. A variety of exercises has been included to both recap and extend the student's knowledge of the techniques involved.

Writing to Describe: Resource Worksheets and OHTs

7c. **'Three Descriptions' Worksheet:** this resource contains three descriptions from Graham Greene's *A Gun for Sale*, describing three different people. Students are asked to pick out key adjectives and verbs from the descriptions to see *how* Greene conveys his impressions.

7d. **'Three Descriptions' OHT:** this is an annotated OHT version of the three descriptions in 7c. 'Three Descriptions' Worksheet. This is for use after the students have completed their task, to compare with their comments.

Writing to Describe: Revision Questions

These six revision questions are for use at your own discretion, for example they could be used for more able students or as homework assignments for exam practice. They cover a range of tasks and topics, for example, describing other people, places or moments in time, your worst fears and a pen-portrait.

1 You are waiting in a bus queue and have been there some time. Describe three or four of the other people who are also waiting.

2 Describe *one* of the following places or moments in time so that they could be easily visualised by a reader:
* a busy railway station
* early morning in a city
* a deserted beach.

3 Describe some of your worst fears, or what would be, for you, a nightmare scenario.

4 Describe a place you know well, in as much detail as possible.

5 Write a pen-portrait of one of your relations, including their individual oddities, in order to 'bring them to life' on the page.

6 Describe a particular place (real or imaginary) at *two* different times of the year or at *two* different times of the day.

7c. THREE DESCRIPTIONS

Look at the following brief descriptions of three characters from Graham Greene's *A Gun for Sale*:

James Raven.

A 'Wanted. James Raven. Aged about twenty-eight. Easily recognisable from his hare-lip. A little above the middle height. Last seen wearing a dark overcoat and a black felt hat . . .'

The 'nurse'.

B 'A woman in nurse's uniform opened the door, a woman with a mean lined face and untidy grey hair. Her uniform needed washing; it was spotted with grease marks and what might have been blood or iodine . . .'

Mr Collier, a pantomime producer.

C 'He was rather undersized with a fierce eye and straw-coloured hair and a receding chin. He was continually glancing over his shoulder in fear that somebody was getting him from behind.'

Each person could be summed up by one of the three words below. Decide which word best fits each description and put the letter (either A, B or C) in the box next to the word.

sinister ☐

dirty ☐

frightened ☐

But how *exactly* does Greene convey this?

Look again at each description in turn. Then underline:

✱ the 'telling' or revealing adjectives

✱ the descriptive verbs (for example, 'glancing').

Your teacher will now show you an OHT of the words you could have underlined. How did you do? Underline any words that you missed.

7d. THREE DESCRIPTIONS

SUSPECTED OF A CRIME	BLACK BIRD OF ILL-OMEN, ASSOCIATED WITH DEATH	DISFIGUREMENT; MAKES HIM DIFFERENT FROM OTHERS

James Raven.

A '*Wanted*. James *Raven*. Aged about twenty-eight. Easily recognisable from his *hare-lip*. A little above the *middle height*. Last seen wearing a *dark* overcoat and a *black* felt hat . . .'

NOT TALL OR IMPOSING	SUGGESTS NIGHT, SECRETS AND DISGUISE	LINKS TO 'RAVEN' AND TO 'DARK'	OLD

WORN, OLD

UNGENEROUS, UNPLEASANT

The 'nurse.'

B 'A woman in nurse's uniform opened the door, a woman with a *mean lined* face and *untidy grey* hair. Her uniform *needed washing*; it was *spotted* with grease marks and what might have been *blood or iodine* . . .'

SIMILAR COLOUR WHEN DRY

UNKEMPT; NURSES ARE USUALLY TIDY

DIRTY; OFF-PUTTING IN A NURSE; LIKELY TO SPREAD INFECTION

WILD, ANGRY

SMALL OR SHORT	UNFLATTERING; WHY NOT 'FAIR' OR 'BLONDE'?

Mr Collier, a pantomime producer.

C 'He was *rather undersized* with a *fierce* eye and *straw-coloured* hair and a *receding* chin. He was *continually glancing* over his shoulder in fear that somebody was getting at him from behind.'

SUGGESTS FEAR OR INSECURITY	SUGGESTS WEAKNESS OF CHARACTER

8 Writing to Analyse, Review, Comment

This part of the 'Writing Triplet' is perhaps the most difficult of the three, although it overlaps, as they all do, with some of the others, for example, analysing an argument or an advertisement. With 'Writing to Analyse' both sides of an argument need to be shown not just one.

Part A: Writing to Analyse

Writing to Analyse: Resource Worksheets and Handouts

8a. 'Analysing an Article – Part 1' Handout: this resource requires students to analyse the article 'Last on the ladder' by Anne Atkins. This resource is a **Higher Tier alternative** to the activities on pages 221–223 of the Student's Book.

Writing to Analyse: Revision Questions

These six revision questions are for use at your own discretion, for example they could be used for more able students or as homework assignments for exam practice. The content of the questions cover analysing key incidents, pros and cons, motives and different sides of a statement or viewpoint.

1. Take a key incident in a book or play which you have read for GCSE and analyse its importance in the whole text.
2. Analyse the pros and cons of living in a new house, rather than an old one.
3. What are the advantages and disadvantages of seeing a much-loved book turned into a film? Use examples such as the BBC adaptation of *Pride and Prejudice* to support your views.
4. Some people believe that it is morally wrong to experiment on laboratory rats, mice or rabbits to find cures for human illnesses. Write an article for your school magazine, examining both sides of the argument.
5. Analyse your own motives and feelings when you did *either* something you were proud of *or* something of which you were ashamed.
6. 'As a nation we prefer pets to people. The RSPCA is a more popular charity than the NSPCC.'
   Examine both sides of this statement and say how far you consider it to be true.

8a. ANALYSING AN ARTICLE – PART 1

Analyse Anne Atkins's attitudes to home ownership, her own mistakes and her future hopes.

last on the ladder

By Anne Atkins

I'm not sure of the exact moment that I realised we'd missed the boat. I don't mean failed to buy one particular house. I mean dished our chances altogether. Failed to buy at all. Never destined to be home-owners. Members of that tiny elite of tenants, vagrants and bench-sleepers who don't have to wince every time there's bad news about interest rates on the *Today* programme.

Shaun says he rather likes it this way. Life is but a journey, he says. To be fair, he's never said anything half as clichéd – but he must have communicated some such sentiment, in rather more sophisticated terms. As we were, then: life is a journey. We are merely sojourners. Ships in the night.

And here are we, he and I, shining examples of travelling carefree and light. In fact, we're travelling so light we forgot even to pack life's overnight bag, let alone a house, so when we get to three score and 10, we'll look down into the grave and hop in gaily, glad to have somewhere to lay our weary heads. Foxes have holes, birds of the air have nests, but the Atkinses are too incompetent to manage even that much.

It sets us aside from the masses: Tony Blair says we're all middle-class now, but you can't be middle-class without your own house, so yah-boo-sucks to that. We are the trendy proletariat; like teenagers, without responsibilities – apart, of course, from the responsibility of having four teenagers ourselves and having to earn a living and being permanently broke, as all parents of teenagers always are.

As I say, I'm not sure when this realisation truly hit me, but I suspect it was about two years ago. When I knew that we should have bought the first house we had an offer on, three years earlier, which never sold. Something told me that we'd blown it, good and proper.

We went on looking, of course. We still get details of properties, even now. But we can't do anything about them because I've finally admitted that we can no longer afford to buy anything we like on the diminishing nest egg we have left, and I've blown it on something else.

My decision has a kind of reckless logic to it. I've always been brought up to be careful with money. Excessively careful. And that is why we don't have a house. Any purchase involves a risk: a small, sensible, calculated risk, but nevertheless a risk. By not chancing it, we have lost tens, perhaps hundreds of

> **'We can no longer afford to buy anything'**

thousands, of pounds. The Cambridge townhouse we could once have bought as students, the Devon farmhouse we could have just managed a few years ago – either would be worth a third of a million quid now. Instead of which we have a perfectly safe and totally useless little pot of money that wouldn't buy a broom cupboard.

Or rather had. The principles I was brought up with, I said to myself, are outdated. If you keep your money absolutely risk-free, like the talent buried in the ground, it reduces itself to the point of worthlessness. And we've lost so much already, by being cautious.

So when my brother – the one who took a huge mortgage and a huge gamble in the 1980s, and is now sitting on a north Oxford goldmine – when my clever brother invented a gadget and founded a company, I expressed interest.

'You could lose everything,' he said.

'I have already,' I said, thinking of the farmhouse.

'Can you afford to?' he asked.

'Can I afford not to? How else can I buy my farmhouse?'

He made it clear. I might never see my money again. Or it might come back to me tenfold. And there you have it. Our savings can't buy or dream, so now they're paying for an innovative little device that can track animals on a mobile phone.

Don't show me any more houses. Not yet. But ask me again in three years' time, and I will either grind my teeth or show you my millionaire's mansion, bought with shares from the famous OxLoc sell-off.

Part B: Writing to Review

Interpreting this as widely as possible, 'Writing to Review' includes considering and reflecting on personal and public matters but also taking a critical overview of books, plays, films, and so on.

Writing to Review: Resource Worksheets and OHTs

8b. **'Nightingale's Review Answers' OHT:** this OHT contains the answers to the questions about Benedict Nightingale's review of 'Daisy Pulls It Off' on page 226 of the Student's Book.

8c. **'Pop Bands Review Answers' OHT:** this OHT contains a completed version of the table on page 227 of the Student's Book. Show this version to the class once they have completed their own tables and ask them to add in any positive or negative comments they might have missed.

8d. **'Two Higher Tier Reviews' Worksheets:** this resource contains two Higher Tier examples of reviews (an opera and a concert) with a question set, which may be done *either* on the pair of review *or* separately.

Writing to Review: Revision Questions

These six revision questions are for use at your own discretion, for example they could be used for more able students or as homework assignments for exam practice. The content of the questions includes reviewing a book or film, advantages and disadvantages and family history.

1 Review a book, film or computer game which you have recently enjoyed.

2 Review the TV programmes that you would watch in an average week.

3 Consider the prospect of your generation living to an average lifespan of 120 years. Review the advantages and disadvantages of living so long.

4 On the basis of current developments in science, medicine and electronics, review what life will be like for the average person by the time you reach retirement age.

5 Review what you know of your family history in the last 50 years and show how it is linked to changes or upheavals in society generally.

6 Write a brief survey of the main changes in your local area during the last few years (for example, new housing, shops or roads, or things closing down).

8b. NIGHTINGALE'S REVIEW ANSWERS

'Jolly Good Return to an Age that Never was' by Benedict Nightingale

1   The play is a period-piece, based on Roedean in the 1920s and the values of the time: patriotism, pluck, modesty and gamesmanship.

2   We learn that Daisy Meredith is 'a scholarship girl from an elementary school'; 'brilliant at work'; 'stunning at games'; 'plucky, modest' and honest. She is initially loathed by her morally weaker social superiors!

3   The reviewer, Nightingale, says he hated games and drank gin secretly. This could possibly be made up!

4   These comments suggest that he found it was so good a production that all his initial reluctance was quickly changed to enjoyment.

5   He means that the play makes great escapist pleasure from a 'past' age.

6   You could use phrases, such as: 'good fun', 'innocent pleasure', 'well produced' and 'worth a visit'.

7   The reviewer uses language from the 1920s, for example, 'gels', 'ripping', 'pash', 'rotter', 'alma mater', 'topping', and so on.

8c. **POP BANDS REVIEW ANSWERS**

Here is a completed version of the table from page 227 of the Student's Book. Add any comments you missed to your own tables.

NAME OF BAND	NEGATIVE COMMENTS	POSITIVE COMMENTS
Lorien	'nul points for the performance'; they 'barely moved a muscle and made no attempt to interact with the audience'.	'lived up to coldplay comparisons'; 'enchanting set'; 'low-key' and 'midtempo' music well mixed; 'full marks for the music'.
Athlete	'Odd, electronic rock'; 'made them sound like a moody XTC'; all songs started 'slow', then 'pick[ed] up speed'; best song was 'Chaotic'.	'slightly more energetic': 'nodding their heads'; 'got the audience to groove along' in song *Beautiful*.
Alfie	'Manchester outfit' with an 'experimental approach'; 'shambolic songs'; their song 'zoom became a guitar-drenched joke'. Ed. Harcourt 40 mins late; very bad dancing/ told silly stories.	Made effort when he got there; looked as though he was enjoying it.

8d. TWO HIGHER TIER REVIEWS

Analyse the tone and balance of positive and negative comment in these two Higher Tier reviews:

A

Concert
LPO / Masur
Festival Hall
★★★☆☆

THIS was a concert in celebration of Kurt Masur's 75th birthday. No one sang, there was no cake, for the day doesn't arrive until the middle of July. But everyone still had reason to be happy. For the London Philharmonic Orchestra's chief conductor was back in business, after an extended period of surgery and recuperation. And he was bringing with him two special presents: Anne-Sophie Mutter, and a new work written for her golden violin by the French master Henri Dutilleux, a mere 86 himself. The hall was sold out.

Festivities began with Beethoven's violin Romances, two pieces with as much muscle as an amoeba but with bags of compensating charm. Swaying gently in the breeze, Mutter conjured from her instrument the fastest vibrato in the west, each note burnished with a little halo. But agility was never affected. With one flick of her bow and fingers, forte became the softest pianissimo. And the second Romance's serene song undulated in a seamless line. An old-fashioned performance, this; but it was what the music required.

Dutilleux's *Sur le même accord* needed extra virtuosity, with multiple effects squeezed into nine minutes. It carries a subtitle, *Nocturne for violin and orchestra*, though in form the work more closely resembles a mini-concerto, and the orchestration's preference for the low and the dark never entirely dominates.

At a first hearing, at least, the piece disappointed. Form and colour appeared less fastidiously worked than usual, though Dutilleux certainly kept busy yanking the six notes of the work's motivating chord up and down and round the houses. Not for nothing does the title translate, approximately, as 'About a Single Chord'. Still, it intrigued, and Mutter and Masur made sure everything fell on the ears gracefully.

Only after the interval did the spotlight land on the maestro and the orchestra alone. The repertoire stayed French – not exactly masur's greatest strength, though the Viennese swirls and hesitations of Ravel's *La Valse* at least got his arms waltzing. Before that came Debussy and *La Mer*, given the tightest, if not the most appropriate, account of the night.

Treacherous things, these seascapes. Only a fine line separates a properly 'impressionist' performance from one that uses the dawn streaks, the sun glinting on the waves and such, as subjects for dry analysis. The LPO, a little lacking in bloom and sheen, stayed just on the line's wrong side. They were wearing white lab coats, not sailor suits. But party hats remain in order: it's good to have Masur back.

Geoff Brown

8d. **TWO HIGHER TIER REVIEWS**

continued

B

Beware of sugar-coated peasant life

Opera
The Kiss
Opera Theatre Company, Dun Laoghaire

★★☆☆☆

SMETANA'S late opera is hardly ever performed, possibly because it is comprensive rubbish, a vastly over-extended anecdote, in itself barely worth the telling, set to cloying, heel-down musical jollities (written when the composer was stone-deaf) and introducing more clichés of peasant life than you care to imagine.

Of course, being opera, none of this need matter much, and *The Kiss* is almost as much *the* Czech national opera as *The Bartered Bride*, and contains many of the same elements of luminous humanity and triumphant romanticism.

Opera Theatre Company, in a severely reduced version (an orchestra of six), made brave attempts to capture the magic of the original but achieved the unique reverse Gestalt of coming up with rather less than the sum of its parts.

The 'plot' concerns the pre-marital tensions generated by Vendulka's refusal to kiss (or 'kiss') her betrothed Lukas out of a hysterical desire not to offend his recently dead first wife. Further psychological complications are introduced by the presence of Lukas's baby, who is passed around among the female characters like a time bomb, and largely abandoned for tracts of Act II. Following the bust-up, Vendulka takes up a sensationally unsuccessful career as a smuggler of tobacco before Lukas sees the indecency of his lustful desires and apologises.

Now the trouble with reducing an opera which relies on the irresistible sweep of its orchestral writing is that it can end up sounding like a polite and bloodless palm-court trio or the theme tune for *Fawlty Towers*. *The Kiss* has plenty of intimate moments, well-conveyed by arranger Mark Armstrong's version for violin, cello, flute, horn and clarinet, with prominent piano accompaniment: sweet moments of gentle rocking to go with Vendulka's lullabies and some with the plain directness of Schumann chamber music. But mostly it just lacked the texture and momentum that can make this often simple-minded music so compelling.

The singing was almost all excellent, only Eugene Ginty's Lukas sounding a little strained and unsupported. *The Kiss* is curious in that the most testing aria is sung by a minor character, played here by Michelle Sheridan who pulled it off radiantly. Virginia Kerr was a soulful Vendulka; Frances McCafferty a rich-voiced and uncaricatured auntie; Andrew Slater his usual impressive presence as Matou. A simple staging, with enough birch-bark implements to stock a Russian souvenir shop, provided few hiding places for some basic acting.

At its best OTC is an outstanding small touring company, with a pleasantly offbeat repertoire and high musical and dramatic standards. So it's a shame to see them doing something which isn't suited to their talents: *The Kiss* may be intimate but it is hardly chamber-opera. If you're not too horrified by the idea of sugar-coated peasant life, with music to match, it's not a bad way of passing an evening. But sceptics of all kinds should beware.

Robert Thicknesse

Part C: Writing to Comment

B

What *isn't* commenting, of one sort or another? The students will therefore have a vast amount of experience of this mode of writing. The sample exam questions focus on personal experience but may widen out to include other forms of commentary at a later date. It is therefore important to use a range of stimulus material on people, places, events, and so on.

Writing to Comment: Revision Questions

These six revision questions are for use at your own discretion, for example they could be used for more able students or as homework assignments for exam practice. They cover a range of writing genre (commentary, mini-guide, letter) for different audiences and purposes and are therefore useful revision exercises.

1 Write a detailed commentary on one or two television programmes that you have watched recently.

2 Your school is revising its Prospectus and students from Years 10 to 13 have been asked to contribute to it. You have been asked to describe and comment on the extra-curricular activities available for Year 10 and Year 11 students.

3 Write a mini-guide for visitors to your town, village or city locality, commenting on facilities (for example, shopping or sports centres), things to see, places to eat, and so on.

4 Describe any sporting event which you have recently seen or taken part in, commenting on its highlights or key moments.

5 Imagine yourself in 50 years' time, looking back on a long and happy life. Write a letter to your grandchildren, commenting on differences between your life when you were young and theirs when they were young and how life generally has changed. Keep the tone positive!

6 Think of an issue on which you have strong feelings (for example, animal rights, religious education, fast food, and so on). Explain your own views and comment on the opposing view and what you think is wrong with it.

9 Pre-1914 Text

The Specifications

The requirements of Pre-1914 Poetry Literature Coursework are as follows:

✱ It must be based on the study of a substantial collection of Pre-1914 poetry, which is defined as about 15–20 shorter poems, or a smaller number of longer poems, linked by theme, poet(s) or form.

✱ The coursework assignment should range across the collection, referring in closer detail to 5–6 poems.

✱ It is important to remember that students whose assignments do not meet these requirements will be penalised.

Assessment Objectives

✱ The focus of this unit is:
  ▶ to enable students to respond critically and sensitively to a range of poems
  ▶ to encourage students to show understanding of how ideas are conveyed through language, structure and form
  ▶ to allow students to make connections and comparisons between poems, supporting their views by detailed references.

✱ As well as meeting the Assessment Objectives above, it is important to remember that:
  ▶ students must demonstrate their ability to relate texts to their social, cultural and historical contexts and literary traditions.

✱ This is worth 10% of the total marks.

There follow several suggested collections of poetry to both meet the assessment criteria and provide for students of all abilities.
Collections A and B have the poems themselves printed as well as the suggested coursework assignments in photocopiable handouts, whilst Collection C just lists the poems and the assignments.

Pre-1914 Poetry: Resource Handouts

Collection A

9Aa. **'Marlowe and Shakespeare' Handout:** this resource contains the poems, 'The Passionate Shepherd to his Love' by Christopher Marlowe and 'Sonnet 116' by William Shakespeare. *See page 177*

9Ab. **'Sidney and Jonson' Handout:** this resource contains the poems, 'My True Love hath my Heart' by Sir Philip Sidney and 'Song. To Celia' by Ben Jonson. *See page 178*

9Ac. **'Marvell' Handout:** this resource contains the poem, 'To His Coy Mistress' by Andrew Marvell. *See page 179*

9Ad. **'Burns and Blake' Handout:** this resource contains the poems, 'A Red, Red Rose' by Robert Burns and 'The Echoing Green' by William Blake. *See page 180*

9Ae. **'Byron' Handout:** this resource contains the poems, 'So We'll Go No More A-Roving' and 'When We Two Parted', both by Lord Byron. *See page 181*

9Af. **'Wordsworth' Handout:** this resource contains the poem, 'Lucy' by William Wordsworth. *See page 182*

9Ag. **'Robert Browning – Part 1' Handout:** this resource contains the poem, 'My Last Duchess' by Robert Browning. *See page 184*

9Ah. **'Robert Browning – Part 2' Handout:** this resource contains the poems, 'Meeting at Night' and 'Parting at Morning', both by Robert Browning. *See page 185*

9Ai. **'Barratt-Browning and Rossetti' Handout:** this resource contains the poems, 'How do I love Thee' by Elizabeth Barratt Browning and 'Remember' by Christina Rossetti. *See page 186*

9Aj. **'Wadsworth Longfellow' Handout:** this resource contains the poem, 'The Children's Hour' by Henry Wadsworth Longfellow. *See page 187*

Collection B

9Bk. **'Blake – Pair 1' Handout:** this resource contains the poems, 'The Lamb' and 'The Tyger'. *See page 189*

9Bl. **'Blake – Pair 2' Handout:** this resource contains the poems, 'The Ecchoing Green' and 'London'. *See page 190*

9Bm. **'Blake – Pair 3' Handout:** this resource contains two poems both entitled 'the Chimney Sweeper'. *See page 191*

9Bn. **'Blake – Pair 4' Handout:** this resource contains the poems, 'The Divine Image' and 'The Human Abstract'. *See page 192*

9Bo. **'Blake – Pair 5' Handout:** this resource contains two poems, both entitled 'Nurse's Song'. *See page 193*

9Bp. **'Blake – Pair 6' Handout:** this resource contains the poems, 'The Blossom' and 'The Sick Rose'. *See page 194*

9Bq. **'Blake – Pair 7' Handout:** this resource contains the poems, 'Infant Joy' and 'Infant Sorrow'. *See page 195*

9Br. **'Blake – Pair 8' Handout:** this resource contains the poems, 'Laughing Song' and 'The Garden of Love'. *See page 196*

Collection A: Relationships

Collection A includes poetry to suit students of all abilities.

WRITING ACTIVITIES

1 Poets down the ages have written about love and relationships, their joys and problems. Compare the different ways and forms in which poets have expressed their sentiments over the centuries.

2 Show how different writers have explored the theme of love in various forms (for example, sonnet, lyric, ode, dramatic monologue).

3 Explore how attitudes to love changed from the times of Marlowe and Shakespeare to those of Browning and Longfellow.

4 Explore the theme of change/loss in these poems, showing how the poets use language and form to express their ideas.

9Aa. MARLOWE AND SHAKESPEARE

1 The Passionate Shepherd to his Love

Come live with me, and be my love,
And we will all the pleasures prove
That valleys, groves, hills and fields,
Woods, or steepy mountain yields.

And we will sit upon the rocks,
Seeing the shepherds feed their flocks
By shallow rivers, to whose falls
Melodious birds sing madrigals.

And I will make thee beds of roses,
And a thousand fragrant posies,
A cap of flowers and a kirtle,
Embroider'd all with leaves of myrtle

A gown made of the finest wool
Which from our pretty lambs we pull,
Fair lined slippers for the cold,
With buckles of the purest gold.

A belt of straw and ivy buds,
With coral clasps and amber studs,
And if these pleasures may thee move,
Come live with me, and be my love.

The shepherd swains shall dance and sing
For thy delight each May-morning.
If these delights thy mind may move,
Then live with me, and be my love.

Christopher Marlowe

2 Sonnet 116

Let me not to the marriage of true minds
Admit impediments. Love is not love
Which alters when it alteration finds,
Or bends with the remover to remove:
O, no! it is an ever-fixed mark,
That looks on tempests and is never shaken;
It is the star to every wandering bark,
Whose worth's unknown, although his height be taken.
Love's not Time's fool, though rosy lips and cheeks
Within his bending sickle's compass come;
Love alters not with his brief hours and weeks,
But bears it out even to the edge of doom.
    If this be error, and upon me prov'd,
    I never writ, nor no man ever lov'd.

William Shakespeare

9Ab. SIDNEY AND JONSON

3 My True Love hath my Heart

My true love hath my heart, and I have his,
By just exchange, one for the other giv'n.
I hold his dear, and mine he cannot miss:
There never was a bargain better driv'n.
His heart in me, keeps me and him in one,
My heart in him, his thoughts and senses guides.
He loves my heart, for once it was his own:
I cherish his, because in me it bides.

His heart his wound received from my sight;
My heart was wounded, with his wounded heart,
For as from me on him his hurt did light,
So still methought in me his hurt did smart;
    Both equal hurt, in this change sought our bliss:
    My true love hath my heart, and I have his.

Sir Philip Sidney

4 Song. To Celia

Come my Celia, let us prove,
While we may, the sports of love;
Time will not be ours, for ever:
He, at length, our good will sever.
Spend not then his gifts in vain.
Suns, that set, may rise again:
But if once we lose this light,
'Tis, with us, perpetual night.
Why should we defer our joys?
Fame, and rumour are but toys.
Cannot we delude the eyes
Of a few poor household spies?
Or his easier ears beguile,
So removéd by our wile?
'Tis no sin, love's fruit to steal,
But the sweet theft to reveal:
To be taken, to be seen,
These have crimes accounted been.

Ben Jonson

9Ac. MARVELL

5 To His Coy Mistress

Had we but world enough, and time,
This coyness, lady, were no crime.
We would sit down and think which way
To walk, and pass our long love's day;
Thou by the Indian Ganges' side
Shouldst rubies find; I by the tide
An age at least to every part
And the last age should show your heart
For, lady, you deserve this state,
Nor would I love at lower rate.
  Of Humber would complain. I would
Love you ten years before the Flood;
And you should, if you please, refuse
  Till the conversion of the Jews.
  My vegetable love should grow
Vaster than empires, and more slow.
An hundred years should go to praise
Thine eyes, and on thy forehead gaze;
Two hundred to adore each breast,
But thirty thousand to the rest;
  But at my back I always hear
Time's winged chariot hurrying near;
And yonder all before us lie
Deserts of vast eternity.

Thy beauty shall no more be found,
Nor, in thy marble vault, shall sound
My echoing song; then worms shall try
That long preserv'd virginity,
  And your quaint honour turn to dust,
And into ashes all my lust.
The grave's a fine and private place,
But none I think do there embrace.
  Now therefore, while the youthful hue
  Sits on thy skin like morning dew,
And while thy willing soul transpires
  At every pore with instant fires,
Now let us sport us while we may;
And now, like amorous birds of prey,
Rather at once our time devour,
  Than languish in his slow-chapp'd power.
Let us roll all our strength, and all
Our sweetness, up into one ball;
And tear our pleasures with rough strife
Thorough the iron gates of life.
Thus, though we cannot make our sun
Stand still, yet we will make him run.

Andrew Marvell

BURNS AND BLAKE

6 A Red, Red Rose

My love is like a red, red rose,
    That's newly sprung in June:
My love is like the melodie,
    That's sweetly play'd in tune.

As fair art thou, my bonnie lass,
    So deep in love am I;
And I will love thee still, my dear,
    Till all the seas gang dry.

Till all the seas gang dry, my dear,
    And the rocks melt wi' the sun;
And I will love thee still, my dear,
    While the sands of life shall run.

And fare-thee-weel, my only love!
    And fare-thee-weel, a while!
And I will come again, my love,
    Tho' 'twere ten thousand mile!

Robert Burns

7 The Echoing green

The sun does arise,
And make happy the skies;
The merry bells ring
To welcome the spring;
The skylark and thrush,
The birds of the bush,
Sing louder around,
To bells' chearful sound,
While our sports shall be seen
On the Echoing Green.

Old John with white hair
Does laugh away care,
Sitting under the oak,
Among the old folk.
They laugh at our play,
And soon they all say,

'Such, such were the joys,
When we all, girls and boys,
In our youth-time were seen
On the Echoing Green.'

Till the little ones weary
No more can be merry;
The sun does descend,
And our sports have an end.
Round the laps of their mothers,
Many sisters and brothers,
Like birds in their nest,
Are ready for rest —
And sport no more seen,
On the darkening Green.

Willliam Blake

BYRON

9Ae.

8 *So, We'll Go No More A Roving*

So, we'll go no more a roving
   So late into the night,
Though the heart be still as loving,
   And the moon be still as bright.

For the sword outwears its sheath,
   And the soul wears out the breast,

And the heart must pause to breathe,
   And love itself have rest.

Though the night was made for loving,
   And the day returns too soon,
Yet we'll go no more a roving
   By the light of the moon.

Lord Byron

9 *When We Two Parted*

When we two parted
   In silence and tears,
Half broken-hearted
   To sever for years,
Paler grew thy cheek and cold,
   Colder thy kiss;
Truly that hour foretold
   Sorrow to this.

The dew of the morning
   Sunk chill on my brow —
It felt like the warning
   Of what I feel now.
Thy vows are all broken,
   And light is thy fame;
I heard thy name spoken,
   And share in its shame.

They name thee before me,
   A knell to mine ear;
A shudder comes o'er me —
   Why wert thou so dear?
They know not I knew thee
   Who knew thee too well: —
Long, long shall I rue thee,
   Too deeply to tell.

In secret we met —
   In silence I grieve,
That they heart could forget,
   Thy spirit deceive.
If I should meet thee
   After long years,
How should I greet thee? —
   With silence and tears.

Lord Byron

9Af.

WORDSWORTH

10 Lucy

I

Strange fits of passion have I known:
And I will dare to tell,
But in the lover's ear alone,
What once to me befell.

When she I loved look'd every day
Fresh as a rose in June,
I to her cottage bent my way,
Beneath an evening moon.

Upon the moon I fix'd my eye,
All over the wide lea;
With quickening pace my horse drew nigh
Those paths so dear to me.

And now we reach'd the orchard-plot;
And, as we climb'd the hill,
The sinking moon to Lucy's cot
Came near and nearer still.

In one of those sweet dreams I slept,
Kind Nature's gentlest boon!
And all the while my eyes I kept
On the descending moon.

My horse moved on; hoof after hoof
He raised, and never stopp'd:
When down behind the cottage roof,
At once, the bright moon dropp'd.

What fond and wayward thoughts will slide
Into a lover's head!
'O mercy!' to myself I cried,
'If Lucy should be dead!'

II

He dwelt among the untrodden ways
Beside the springs of Dove,
A Maid whom there were none to praise
And very few to love:

A violet by a mossy stone
Half hidden from the eye!
Fair as a star, when only one
Is shining in the sky.

She lived unknown, and few could know
When Lucy ceased to be;
But she is in her grave, and oh,
The difference to me!

III

Travell'd among unknown men,
In lands beyond the sea;
Nor, England! did I know till then
What love I bore to thee.

'Tis past, that melancholy dream!
Nor will I quit thy shore
A second time; for still I seem
To love thee more and more.

Among the mountains did I feel
The joy of my desire;
And she I cherish'd turn'd her wheel
Beside an English fire.

Thy mornings show'd, thy nights conceal'd,
The bowers where Lucy play'd;
And thine too is the last green field
That Lucy's eyes survey'd.

9Af. WORDSWORTH

continued

IV

Three years she grew in sun and shower;
Then Nature said, 'A lovelier flower
On earth was never sown;
This child I to myself will take;
She shall be mine, and I will make
A lady of my own.

'Myself will to my darling be
Both law and impulse; and with me
The girl, in rock and plain,
In earth and heaven, in glade and bower,
Shall feel an overseeing power
To kindle or restrain.

'She shall be sportive as the fawn
That wild with glee across the lawn
Or up the mountain springs;
And hers shall be the breathing balm,
And hers the silence and the calm
Of mute insensate things.

'The floating clouds their state shall lend
To her; for her the willow bend;
Nor shall she fail to see
Even in the motions of the storm
Grace that shall mould the maiden's form
By silent sympathy.

'The stars of midnight shall be dear
To her; and she shall lean her ear
In many a secret place
Where rivulets dance their wayward round,
And beauty born of murmuring sound
Shall pass into her face.

'And vital feelings of delight
Shall rear her form to stately height,
Her virgin bosom swell;
Such thoughts to Lucy I will give
While she and I together live
Here in this happy dell.'

Thus Nature spake – The work was done –
How soon my Lucy's race was run!
She died, and left to me
This heath, this calm and quiet scene;
The memory of what has been,
And never more will be.

V

Slumber did my spirit seal;
I had no human fears:
She seem'd a thing that could not feel
The touch of earthly years.

No motion has she now, no force;
She neither hears nor sees;
Roll'd round in earth's diurnal course,
With rocks, and stones, and trees.

William Wordsworth

9Ag. ROBERT BROWNING – PART 1

11 My Last Duchess

That's my last Duchess painted on the wall,
Looking as if she were alive. I call
That piece a wonder, now: Frà Pandolf's hands
Worked busily a day, and there she stands.
Will't please you sit and look at her? I said
'Frà Pandolf' by design, for never read
Strangers like you that pictured countenance,
The depth and passion of its earnest glance,
But to myself they turned (since none puts by
The curtain I have drawn for you, but I)
And seemed as they would ask me, if they durst,
How such a glance came there; so, not the first
Are you to turn and ask thus. Sir, 'twas not
Her husband's presence only, called that spot
Of joy into the Duchess' cheek: perhaps
Frà Pandolf chanced to say 'Her mantle laps
Over my lady's wrist too much,' or 'Paint
Must never hope to reproduce the faint
Half-flush that dies along her throat:' such stuff
Was courtesy, she thought, and cause enough
For calling up that spot of joy. She had
A heart – how shall I say? – too soon made glad,
Too easily impressed; she liked whate'er
She looked on, and her looks went everywhere.
Sir, 'twas all one! My favour at her breast,
The dropping of the daylight in the West,
The bough of cherries some officious fool
Broke in the orchard for her, the white mule
She rode with round the terrace – all and each
Would draw from her alike the approving
                                                    speech,
Or blush, at least. She thanked men, – good! but
                                                    thanked

Somehow – I know not how – as if she ranked
My gift of a nine-hundred-years-old name
With anybody's gift. Who'd stoop to blame
This sort of trifling? Even had you skill
In speech – (which I have not) – to make your
                                                    will
Quite clear to such an one, and say, 'Just this
Or that in you disgusts me; here you miss,
Or there exceed the mark' – and if she let
Herself be lessoned so, nor plainly set
Her wits to yours, forsooth, and made excuse,
– E'en then would be some stooping; and I
                                                    choose
Never to stoop. Oh sir, she smiled, no doubt,
Whene'er I passed her; but who passed without
Much the same smile? This grew; I gave
                                                    commands;
Then all smiles stopped together. There she
                                                    stands
As if alive. Will't please you rise? We'll meet
The company below, then. I repeat,
The Count your master's known munificence
Is ample warrant that no just pretence
Of mine for dowry will be disallowed;
Though his fair daughter's self, as I avowed
At starting, is my object. Nay, we'll go
Together down, sir. Notice Neptune, though,
Taming a sea-horse, thought a rarity,
Which Claus of Innsbruck cast in bronze for
                                                    me!
Robert Browning

ROBERT BROWNING – PART 2

12 Meeting at Night

The grey sea and the long black land;
And the yellow half-moon large and low;
And the startled little waves that leap
In fiery ringlets from their sleep,
As I gain the cove with pushing prow,   5
And quench its speed i' the slushy sand.

Then a mile of warm sea-scented beach;
Three fields to cross till a farm appears;
A tap at the pane, the quick sharp scratch
And blue spurt of a lighted match,   10
And a voice less loud, through its joys and fears,
Than the two hearts beating each to each!

Robert Browning

13 Parting at Morning

Round the cape of a sudden came the sea,
And the sun looked over the mountain's rim:
And straight was a path of gold for him,
And the need of a world of men for me.

Robert Browning

9Ai. **BARRETT-BROWNING AND ROSSETTI**

14 How do I love Thee?

How do I love thee? Let me count the ways! —
I love thee to the depth & breadth & height
My soul can reach, when feeling out of sight
For the ends of Being and Ideal Grace.
I love thee to the level of everyday's
Most quiet need, by sun & candlelight—
I love thee freely, as men strive for Right,—
I love thee purely, as they turn from Praise;
I love thee with the passion, put to use
In my old griefs, . . . and with my childhood's faith:
I love thee with a love I seemed to lose
With my lost Saints, — I love with the breath,
Smiles, tears, of all my life! — and, if God choose,
I shall but love thee better after death.

Elizabeth Barrett-Browning

15 Remember

Remember me when I am gone away,
    Gone far away into the silent land;
    When you can no more hold me by the hand,
Nor I half turn to go yet turning stay.
Remember me when no more day by day
    You tell me of our future that you plann'd:
    Only remember me; you understand
It will be late to counsel then or pray.
Yet if you should forget me for a while
    And afterwards remember, do not grieve:
    For if the darkness and corruption leave
    A vestige of the thoughts that I once had,
Better by far you should forget and smile
    Than that you should remember and be sad.

Christina Rossetti

9Aj. WADSWORTH LONGFELLOW

16 The Children's Hour

Between the dark and the daylight,
    When the night is beginning to lower,
Comes a pause in the day's occupations,
    That is known as the Children's Hour.

I hear in the chamber above me
    The patter of little feet,
The sound of a door that is opened,
    And voices soft and sweet.

From my study I see in the lamplight,
    Descending the broad hall stair,
Grave Alice, and laughing Allegra,
    And Edith with golden hair.

A whisper, and then a silence:
    Yet I know by their merry eyes
They are plotting and planning together
    To take me by surprise.

A sudden rush from the stairway,
    A sudden raid from the hall!
By three doors left unguarded
    They enter my castle wall!

They climb up into my turret
    O'er the arms and back of my chair;
If I try to escape, they surround me;
    They seem to be everywhere.

They almost devour me with kisses,
    Their arms about me entwine,
Till I think of the Bishop of Bingen
    In his Mouse-Tower on the Rhine!

Do you think, O blue-eyed banditti,
    Because you have scaled the wall,
Such an old mustache as I am
    Is not a match for you all!

I have you fast in my fortress,
    And will not let you depart,
But put you down into the dungeon
    In the round-tower of my heart.

And there will I keep you forever,
    Yes, forever and a day,
Till the walls shall crumble to ruin,
    And moulder in dust away!
                    Henry Wadsworth Longfellow

Collection B: A Selection of Blake's 'Songs of Innocence and Experience'

The poems in this collection represent a Higher Tier Option.

WRITING ACTIVITIES

1 How does Blake use 'Songs of Innocence and Experience' to express his views about the society of his day and its institutions (for example, the Church, education, parenting, child labour)?

2 How and why does Blake express quite complicated ideas in seemingly simple language and verse forms?

BLAKE – PAIR 1

The Lamb

Little Lamb, who made thee?
Dost thou know who made thee?
Gave thee life, and bid thee feed
By the stream and o'er the mead;
Gave thee clothing of delight,
Softest clothing, wooly, bright;
Gave thee such a tender voice,
Making all the vales rejoice?
Little Lamb, who made thee:
Dost though know who made thee?

Little Lamb, I'll tell thee,
Little Lamb, I'll tell thee:
He is called by thy name,
For he calls himself a Lamb.
He is meek, and he is mild;
He became a little child.
I a child, and thou a lamb,
We are called by his name,
Little Lamb, God bless thee!
Little Lamb, God bless thee!

The Tyger

Tyger! Tyger! burning bright
In the forests of the night,
What immortal hand or eye
Could frame thy fearful symmetry?

In what distant deeps or skies
Burnt the fire of thine eyes?
On what wings dare he aspire?
What the hand dare sieze the fire?

And what shoulder, and what art,
Could twist the sinews of thy heart?
And when thy heart began to beat,
What dread hand? and what dread feet?

What the hammer? what the chain?
In what furnace was thy brain?
What the anvil? what dread grasp
Dare its deadly terrors clasp?

When the stars threw down their spears,
And water'd heaven with their tears,
Did he smile his work to see?
Did he who made the Lamb make thee?

Tyger! Tyger! burning bright
In the forests of the night,
What immortal hand or eye
Dare frame thy fearful symmetry?

9Bl.   BLAKE – PAIR 2

The Echoing Green

The sun does arise,
And make happy the skies;
The merry bells ring
To welcome the spring;
The skylark and thrush,
The birds of the bush,
Sing louder around,
To bells' chearful sound,
While our sports shall be seen
On the Echoing Green.

Old John with white hair
Does laugh away care,
Sitting under the oak,
Among the old folk.
They laugh at our play,

And soon they all say,
'Such, such were the joys,
When we all, girls and boys,
In our youth time were seen
On the Echoing Green.'

Till the little ones weary
No more can be merry;
The sun does descend,
And our sports have an end.
Round the laps of their mothers,
Many sisters and brothers,
Like birds in their nest,
Are ready for rest—
And sport no more seen,
On the darkening Green.

London

I wander thro' each charter'd street,
Near where the charter'd Thames does flow,
And mark in every face I meet
Marks of weakness, marks of woe.

In every cry of every Man,
In every Infant's cry of fear,
In every voice, in every ban,
The mind-forg'd manacles I hear.

How the Chimney-sweeper's cry
Every black'ning Church appalls;
And the hapless Soldier's sigh
Runs in blood down Palace walls.

But most thro' midnight streets I hear
How the youthful Harlot's curse
Blasts the new born Infant's tear,
And blights with plagues the Marriage hearse.

BLAKE – PAIR 3

The Chimney Sweeper

When my mother died I was very young,
And my Father sold me while yet my tongue
Could scarcely cry '' 'weep! 'weep! 'weep!'
So your chimneys I sweep, and in soot I sleep.

There's little Tom Dacre, who cried when his head,
That curl'd like a lamb's back, was shav'd: so I said
'Hush Tom! Never mind it, for when your head's bare
'You know that the soot cannot spoil your white hair.'

And so he was quiet, and that very night
As Tom was a-sleeping, he had such a sight!
That thousands of sweepers, Dick, Joe, Ned, and Jack,
Were all of them lock'd up in coffins of black.

And by came an Angel who had a bright key,
And he open'd the coffins and set them all free;
Then down a green plain leaping, laughing, they run,
And wash in a river, and shine in the Sun.

The Naked and white, all their bags left behind,
They rise upon clouds and sport in the wind;
And the Angel told Tom, if he'd be a good boy,
He'd have God for a father, and never want joy.

And so Tom awoke; and we rose in the dark,
And got with our bags and our brushes to work.
Tho' the morning was cold, Tom was happy and warm;
So if all do their duty they need not fear harm.

The Chimney Sweeper

A little black thing among the snow,
Crying '' 'weep! 'weep!' in notes of woe!
'Where are thy father and mother? Say?'
'They are both gone up to the church to pray.

'Because I was happy upon the heath,
'And smil'd among the winter's snow,
'They clothed me in the clothes of death,

'And taught me to sing the notes of woe.

'And because I am happy and dance and sing,
'They think they have done me no injury,
'And are gone to praise God and his Priest and
                                              King,
'Who make up a heaven of our misery.'

9Bn.

BLAKE – PAIR 4

The Divine Image

To Mercy, Pity, Peace, and Love
All pray in their distress;
And to these virtues of delight
Return their thankfulness.

For Mercy, Pity, Peace, and Love
Is God, our Father dear,
And Mercy, Pity, Peace, and Love
Is Man, his child and care.

For Mercy has a human heart,
Pity a human face,
And Love, the human form divine,
And Peace, the human dress.

Then every man, of every clime,
That prays in his distress,
Prays to the human form divine,
Love, Mercy, Pity, Peace.

And all must love the human form,
In heathen, turk or jew;
Where Mercy, Love and Pity dwell
There God is dwelling too.

The Human Abstract

Pity would be no more
If we did not make somebody Poor;
And Mercy no more could be
If all were as happy as we.

And mutual fear brings peace,
Till the selfish loves increase:
Then Cruelty knits a snare,
And spreads his baits with care.

He sits down with holy fears,
And waters the ground with tears;
Then Humility takes its root
Underneath his foot.

Soon spreads the dismal shade
Of Mystery over his head;
And the Catterpiller and Fly
Feed on the Mystery.

And it bears the fruit of Deceit,
Ruddy and sweet to eat;
And the Raven his nest has made
In its thickest shade.

The Gods of the earth and sea
Sought thro' Nature to find this Tree;
But their search was all in vain:
There grows one in the Human Brain.

9Bo. BLAKE – PAIR 5

Nurse's Song

When the voices of children are heard on the green
And laughing is heard on the hill,
My heart is at rest within my breast
    And everything else is still.

"Then come home, my children, the sun is gone down
"And the dews of night arise;
Come, come, leave off play, and let us away
"Till the morning appears in the skies."

"No, no let us play, for it is yet day
"And we cannot go to sleep;
"Besides, in the sky the little birds fly
"And the hills are all cover'd with sheep."

"Well, well, go and play till the light fades away
"And then go home to bed."
The little ones leaped and shouted and laughed
 And all the hills ecchoed.

Nurse's Song

When the voices of children are heard on the green
And whisp'rings are in the dale,
The days of my youth rise fresh in my mind,
My face turns green and pale.

Then come home, my children, the sun is gone down,
And the dews of night arise;
Your spring and your day are wasted in play,
And your winter and night in disguise.

9Bp. BLAKE – PAIR 6

The Blossom

Merry, Merry Sparrow!
Under leaves so green
A happy Blossom
Sees you swift as arrow
Seek your cradle narrow
Near my Bosom.

Pretty, Pretty Robin!
Under leaves so green
A happy Blossom
Hears you sobbing, sobbing,
Pretty, Pretty Robin,
Near my Bosom.

The Sick Rose

O Rose, thou are sick!
The invisible worm
That flies in the night,
In the howling storm,

Has found out thy bed
Of crimson joy:
And his dark secret love
Does thy life destroy.

9Bq.

BLAKE – PAIR 7

Infant Joy

"I have no name:
"I am but two days old."
What shall I call thee?
"I happy am,
"Joy is my name."
Sweet joy befall thee!

Pretty joy!
Sweet joy but two days old,
Sweet joy I call thee:
Thou dost smile,
I sing the while,
Sweet joy befall thee!

Infant Sorrow

My mother groan'd! my father wept.
Into the dangerous world I leapt:
Helpless, naked, piping loud:
Like a fiend hid in a cloud.

Struggling in my father's hands,
Striving against my swaddling bands,
Bound and weary I thought best
To sulk upon my mother's breast.

BLAKE – PAIR 8

Laughing Song

When the green woods laugh with voice of joy,
And the dimpling stream runs laughing by;
When the air does laugh with our merry wit,
And the green hill laughs with the noise of it;

When the meadows laugh with lively green,
And the grasshopper laughs in the merry scene,
When Mary and Susan and Emily
With their sweet round mouths sing 'Ha, Ha! He!'

When the painted birds laugh in the shade,
Where our table with cherries and nuts is spread,
Come live and be merry, and join with me,
To sing the sweet chorus of 'Ha, Ha, He!'

The Garden of Love

I went to the Garden of Love,
And saw what I never had seen:
A Chapel was built in the midst,
Where I used to play on the green.

And the gates of this Chapel were shut,
And 'Thou shalt not' writ over the door;
So I turn'd to the Garden of Love
That so many sweet flowers bore;

And I saw it was filled with graves,
And tomb-stones where flowers should be;
And Priest in black gowns were walking their rounds,
And binding with briars my joys and desires.

Collection C: The Poet and the Natural World

The poems in this collection represent a Foundation Tier option.

The Poems

Blake	'The Echoing Green' 'The Tyger' 'The Lamb'
Clare	'Autumn'
Hardy	'The Darkling Thrush'
Herrick	'To Daffodils'
Hopkins	'Pied Beauty' 'Spring'
Housman	'Loveliest of Trees' (from *A Shropshire Lad*)
Rossetti, C.	'In the Bleak Midwinter'
Shelley	'Summer and Winter'
Tennyson	'The Eagle'
Wordsworth	'I wandered lonely as a cloud' 'March'

WRITING ACTIVITIES

1. From the poems you have studied, show how poets in different times have expressed their thoughts and feelings about nature.

2. Many poets have found peace and consolation in nature, but others have seen a darker, more frightening side to it. Show how the poets you have studied have dealt with these two aspects of nature.

3. How have the poets you have studied used language and form to celebrate the different seasons in their poems?

PROSE

The Specifications

The requirements of the Pre-1914 Prose Literature Coursework are:

✱ It must be based on the work of any major writer/s published before 1914.*

✱ The texts chosen must be of a substantial nature.

✱ Where short stories are used, there should be at least 5–6, which may be linked by a common theme or writer.

✱ Knowledge of the *whole* written *text* must be shown, not just extracts or a media version.

✱ Imaginative/empathic responses or more critical approaches are equally valid, so long as they meet the main requirements.

Assessment objectives

✱ AO1 Respond to texts critically, sensitively and in detail selecting appropriate ways to convey their response, using textual evidence as appropriate.

✱ AO2 Explore how language, structure and forms contribute to the meanings of texts, considering different approaches to texts and alternative interpretations.

✱ AO3 Explore relationships and comparisons between texts, selecting and evaluating relevant material.

✱ AO4 Relate texts to their social, cultural and historical contexts and literary traditions.

For this unit, the emphasis is on AO2 and AO4.

There follow here several suggested texts and assignments to both meet the assessment criteria and provide for students of all abilities.

This is worth 10% of the marks.

* See the National Curriculum Heritage Writers for guidance.

ASSIGNMENTS BASED ON NOVELS

Pride and Prejudice and Emma by Jane Austen

Higher Tier:

✱ How does Jane Austen show different aspects of pride and its consequences in *Pride and Prejudice* and *Emma*?

✱ How does Jane Austen reveal the snobbery and hypocrisy of the society of her day in either *Emma* or *Pride and Prejudice*?

✱ Show the effectiveness of Jane Austen's irony in her portrayal of Mr Collins and Lady Catherine de Bourgh.

Either Tier:

✱ Show how Emma Woodhouse's 'tendency to think a little too well of herself' causes troubles for herself and others.

✱ Imagine that you are Harriet Smith. Write her views of Emma at 3–4 key moments in the story (e.g. when she has just met Emma, after she rejects Robert Martin's proposal, after Mr Elton's marriage, etc.).

Foundation Tier:

✱ How does Mr Knightley show his constant affection for Emma and why is she so slow to see it?

Jane Eyre by Charlotte Brontë

Either Tier

✱ How does Charlotte Brontë succeed in conveying childhood terrors in the first third of *Jane Eyre*?

The Mayor of Casterbridge by Thomas Hardy

Higher Tier:

✱ How does Michael Henchard fit in to the literary tradition of the flawed hero?

✱ Examine the theme of social ambition in *The Mayor of Casterbridge*.

The Hound of the Baskervilles by Sir A. Conan Doyle

Either Tier:

✱ How does Doyle convey an atmosphere of mystery and suspense in *The Hound of the Baskervilles*?

Oliver Twist by Charles Dickens

Higher Tier:

✱ What does Dickens have to say about the poverty and crime of his own time in *Oliver Twist*?

Foundation Tier:

✱ What does the character of Fagin add to *Oliver Twist*?

✱ What do we learn about the lives of orphans in Victorian England from *Oliver Twist*?

A Christmas Carol by Charles Dickens and Silas Marner by George Eliot

Either Tier:

✱ Show how the central characters are transformed by their experiences in to 'better' people in these Victorian novels and suggest what the writers' intentions might have been.

ASSIGNMENTS BASED ON SHORT STORES

The Signalman and *The Black Veil*, by Charles Dickens *The Withered Arm* and *The Melancholy Hussar*, by Thomas Hardy; *The Dream Woman* by Wilkie Collins; *The Monkey's Paw* by W.W. Jacobs; *The Yellow Wallpaper* by C.P. Gilman.

Higher Tier:

✳ Show how the writers depict Victorian attitudes to poverty, madness and crime in any 3–4 of these stories.

✳ Explore the role of or attitudes to women, as depicted in 3–4 of these stories: *The Melancholy Hussar*; *The Withered Arm*; *The Dream Woman*; *The Yellow Wallpaper*; *The Monkey's Paw*.

✳ Analyse how the writers successfully use aspects of the supernatural to create suspense and dramatic tension in any 3–4 of these stories.

✳ How do the writers make effective use of moral dilemmas in: *The Withered Arm*; *The Money's Paw*; *The Signalman*; *The Melancholy Hussar*?

Either Tier:

✳ How are the issues of justice and punishment developed in: *The Withered Arm*; *The Melancholy Hussar*; *The Black Veil*?

✳ Analyse the importance of atmosphere and setting in: *The Signalman*; *The Monkey's Paw*; *The Dream Woman*.

✳ Discuss the theme of 'love and loss' in:
The Withered Arm; *The Monkey's Paw*; *The Melancholy Hussar*.

✳ Discuss the role of dreams or premonitions in any three of the stories.

✳ What is the importance of timing and coincidence in:
The Signalman; *The Dream Woman*; *The Withered Arm*?

✳ Consider the endings of the stories in this collection. Pick out the *two* which you find the most satisfactory and the *two* you find least satisfactory. Explain your reasons.

Foundation Tier:

✳ Explain how atmosphere and setting are important in:
The Signalman and *The Black Veil*.

✳ Explain the 'curious circumstances' in *The Signalman* and *The Monkey's Paw* and how the writers use them to capture and keep the reader's interest.

✳ What do the lives of Phyllis in *The Melancholy Hussar* and the unnamed wife in *The Yellow Wallpaper* tell us about the treatment of women in the mid-19th century?

✳ What does a strong sense of colour add to *The Signalman* (red), *The Black Veil* and *The Yellow Wallpaper*?

Note that all these short stories appear in *Pre-twentieth Short Stories* by Jean Moore and John Catron (Hodder and Stoughton 1999, 0340 73742 5).